Where Life Falls

A Memoir

A.R. (TAS) BROWNING

Published in Australia by Sid Harta Publishers Pty Ltd,
ABN: 34 632 585 203
17 Coleman Parade, GLEN WAVERLEY VIC 3150 Australia
Telephone: +61 3 9560 9920, Facsimile: +61 3 9545 1742
E-mail: author@sidharta.com.au

First published in Australia 2020
This edition published 2020
Edited by Karen Beattie
Copyright © A.R. (Tas) Browning 2020

Cover design, typesetting: WorkingType (www.workingtype.com.au)

The right of A.R. (Tas) Browning to be identified as the Author of the Work has been asserted in accordance with the Copyright, Designs and Patents Act 1988.

All rights reserved. No part of this publication may be reproduced, stored in a retrieval system, or transmitted, in any form or by any means without the prior written permission of the publisher, nor be otherwise circulated in any form of binding or cover other than that in which it is published and without a similar condition being imposed on the subsequent purchaser.

A.R. (Tas) Browning
Where Life Falls
ISBN: 978-1-925707-31-1
pp204

I started to write this biography many years ago with very little knowledge of what was required for the art of writing.

Along the way, I found myself joining up with a local writer's group and I found their knowledge much greater than mine, hence from my first lesson I found friendship as well with many helpers.

I learnt a lot from this group and this has enabled me to give real meaning to my life experiences which the reader's will see.

One cannot go through life without having family, friends and mates to rely on and be given a lift up when needed.

I also need to give my thanks to the many people that did some heavy lifting especially everyone in the medical fraternity who were there when my life needed a lift up.

My father and mother's wedding, early 1930s.

Adam Slater (grandson), self, Paul Hodgkinson, Jim Bush, Mike Keogh

Top (L to R) Chook Fowler, Knobby Clark, Ian Howard, Alan Knudson. Bottom (L to R) : Tom Kiven, Baldy Newcolm, ?, Wilber Forrest, Barry Plester, Self

1970's Naval Reunion East Coast Tasmania
L-R. Self, ?, Late Sir Richard Peck, Late Ron Holmes

Great grandson Eliga Slater at a Naval commemorative service at the Ulverstone RSL October 2018.

Tas on fishing boat, at Scamander in Tasmania, 1975.

Tas cutting cake at 70th birthday with many family and friends

From left: Joan, Faye, Darrell, Tas, Valerie, Anthony.

Jenny's side party, Hong Kong, 1961

Harry's Cafe de Wheels, 1963, near Garden Island

Tas on his way to joining up, late 1958.

Grade Six, Glenora Area School, 1951 Tasmania

20,000 landings on the HMAS Melbourne, 1963

Buster, 2017.

DEFENCE FORCE WELFARE ASSOCIATION

THE UNIQUE NATURE OF MILITARY SERVICE

*This is a shortened version of a full paper
that is available on the DFWA website www.dfwa.org.au*

In recent years there has been a shift in assumptions and attitudes underpinning the way military service is viewed. Those in government who shape policy are increasingly attracted to the idea that the soldier (sailor or airman) is adequately provided for by salary and allowances that compensate for his service both while it is being given and after it has ceased. Military service can be mistakenly seen as comparable to other forms of service that involve risk and danger, and therefore no longer viewed as unique.

The unique nature of military service is rooted in the nature of society itself. Most democratic societies recognize the central place of the individual as the primary unit of sovereignty. Sovereign individuals are vested with inalienable human rights, recognized in the Universal Declaration of Human Rights as, among others, life, liberty and the security of the person (Article 3). Australia is a signatory of the Declaration, adopted by the General Assembly of the UN in 1948

Implicit in Article 3, there is also a right to defence of self and of others from attack, and this right inevitably gives rise to an obligation to do so if it is the State which is under threat or attack.

The inter-relationship of rights and responsibilities borne both by the state and the individual, is complex, and based on the principle of the social contract. The state may not alienate the rights of the individual without that person's assent. The individual, while preserving the integrity of his or her rights, may assent to the state's demand for surrender of some of them for the common good, but in all circumstances save one, the state is obliged to uphold and defend the individual's rights.

In volunteering for military service, the individual accepts the surrender of his basic rights under Article 3. He places his life, liberty and security of person in the hands of the state. This surrender is not unconditional, though *in extremis*, it is absolute. The state, for its part, accepts the obligation to preserve, as far as is consistent with the achievement of the military mission, the physical and spiritual wellbeing of such individuals who place themselves at its disposal. This obligation extends beyond the period of service itself, to the physical and psychological consequences of that service.

Even when the state demands surrender of these rights by imposing a compulsion for service, the terms of the social contract imply that such compulsion is done only within the democratic framework and is therefore with the assent of the individual, who at all times is party to it.

In no other calling, occupation or profession has the state the power to accept or demand the surrender of these rights. Military service in this fundamental respect is unique, and the obligation this places on the state is inescapable, as it is enduring.

A service person's calling is unique.

THE NAVAL ODE

THEY HAVE NO GRAVE
BUT THE CRUEL SEA
NO FLOWERS LAY AT THEIR HEAD
A RUSTING HULK IS THEIR TOMBSTONE
AFAST ON THE OCEAN BED

THEY SHALL GROW NOT OLD
AS WE THAT ARE LEFT GROW OLD
AGE SHALL NOT WEARY THEM
NOR THE YEARS CONDEMN
AT THE GOING DOWN OF THE SUN
AND IN THE MORNING
WE WILL REMEMBER THEM

LEST WE FORGET

IN MEMORY OF ALL OUR SHIPMATES
WHO HAVE GONE ON BEFORE
AND NOW REST IN THE BOSOM
OF THE GREAT MARINER

Foreword

I have been encouraged to tell more of my life, both during the time of the first edition and since that time.

My first book was launched in 2006. I made the mistake of rushing all facets of it and the end result was that there were glaring faults in it: a very quick learning curve. This time around, I have learnt to be patient with all that I do. Sometimes I have had to rely on just my memory instead of old diaries; a diary is something that I have only kept for the last 20 years or so.

In 2010, I saw an advertisement in the local newspaper for a writers' course to be held at the Adult Education rooms here in Devonport, so I registered. At the first group session I was surprised at the mixture of the people attending. Some wrote poetry, some wrote short stories and others a mixture of both. I guess I was naïve in that I had little knowledge of either, but with Faye Forbes leading the workshop, I began to grasp the fundamentals of their work. What transpired out of it was that Faye suggested that I badly needed an editor for my work and I agreed with her. She suggested Karen Beattie as a great source of input as well as the editing and she was right. I would also like to thank Judi McCoy for allowing me to use her poem, *A Day to Remember*. For me, it is exactly as ANZAC Day should be. The group has, for some years, gathered their work and put it into a book, and this year we had a public launch in Devonport. The first page of my research into the naval role into the British atomic tests on the Monte Bello Islands, titled *Chant from Monte Bello* was my contribution; I should add also that I seem to have opened a can of worms!

I hope that you will enjoy the story. I am told it is somewhat unique and one that has given me both joy and sadness. I often look back at the sea of faces that I began my service with and remember those that for many reasons never got to fulfil their obligations to serve out their time in the Navy. Some died in the collision with *HMAS Voyager* and many of the others died in car and motorbike accidents, as well as other service and non-service-related incidents. The cemetery at Nowra in New South Wales is testament to the many who did not survive.

A Day to Remember

By Judi McCoy

Icy chill fills the air
People gathered in coats and hats
Folding arms, hands in pockets
Voices hushed, sombre looks
Young girl stands to speak
Wise words from one so young
Depths of understanding in her voice
Young men dressed in uniform
Stand to attention so still
With barely a blink of their eyes
Older men speak with care
Reminding us of sacrifices made
The hauntingly beautiful Last Post
Plays out among the trees
Moving one and all with pride
Heads bowed solemnly
A silent moment to reflect
Old men's eyes glisten in the dawn
Icy chill fills the air
Lest We Forget.

Dedication

I would like to make this a dedication to many of those that I served with, as I'm sure that without them I would be of some other life somewhere out there. Mateship has been the key to my sometime uneven level of sanity. Just to be able to talk with another veteran is special because of the connection we share. I am glad for the friendships that have endured to the present day, and I give them the value that they deserve.

Mateship is very special; I would call it an emotion that never stops growing and the reward from the harvest is the sincerity that makes it all happen.

I apologise here and now as I am sure that of all the good people listed below, some will have passed on and some will have their rank wrong; my motives are only to thank these people. Their link to me may only be very small, but somewhere along the way they have influenced my life in some way or other.

Admiral Sir Victor Smith AC KBE DSC RAN Rtd. 1913-1998
Late Vice Admiral Sir Richard Peek KBE CB DSC RAN.
Cdr. Gordon McPhee OBE RAN Rtd. 1924-2002
Commodore A.T. (Toz) Dadswell AM RAN Rtd.
Late Cdr. John P. van Gelder RAN.
LCDR. (Shady) Lane RAN Rtd.
LCDR. Ken Douglas RAN Rtd.
LCDR. (Bill) Callan. RAN Rtd.
LCDR. Martin Scott RAN Rtd.
Late LCDR. Alex Ignatieff RAN.
LCDR Keith Stopford RAN Rtd.
LCDR George Mackenzie RAN Rtd.
Lt. (Dusty) King RAN Rtd
Lt. John Elliott RAN Rtd.
Lt. (Steve) Smith RAN Rtd.
Lt. (Knobby) Hall RAN Rtd.
Warrant Officer Neville Russell 15/3/26 – 5/12/99
WO George Plant RAN Rtd.

Lew Petifer	Jack Finch.
Eric Bush	Bill Gardner
'Baldy' Dobson	Ron Melville
Blue Larter	Martin Ward.
George Wilcox	Les Jordan
Late Tom McGuire	Alan Leslie
Dave Laird	Ross Whylie
Ron Forrest	Late Harry Jenkins
George Blondell	Arthur (Butch) Jenkins

Dedication

George Hunt	Ron Jesse
Leo Kirkman	Late Trevor Chatterton
Slim Smith	Fred Olinga
Graeme Campbell	John Ward
Ken Kennedy	Ken Hammond
Late Brian Parrotte	Allen McGowan
Brian Henderson-Smith	Ben Cropley
Bob Johnston	Late Pat Franklin
Bob Gilmour	John Mulhall
Ben Cropley	Geoff Singline
Late Lynton Ferguson	Alf Moffatt
E (Pincher) Martin	David Terry
Late Ron Holmes	George Mills
Barry Arthur	Late Roger Itchens
Spence Sell	Durbin Cooper
Leon O'Donnell	Laurence O'Donnell
Warren Fowler	Barry Plester
Allan Knudson	Tom Kiver
Allan (Knobby) Clark	Vince Nolan
Late 'Cowboy' Keating	David Tomkinson
Rod Venning	Kevin Whitting
Tony Halpin	Joe Linacher
Late Bill Paul	Late Lyle (Pop) Stark
Late Warren Donahue	Late Barry Fallon
Late John Isherwood	Late James (Whiskey) Dalton
Late Charlie O'Farrell	Late Keith (Baron) Kettley

In addition to this, the following people have been very helpful in my research efforts and should be thanked too:
Department of Veterans' Affairs
Australian War Memorial
National Archives of Australia
UK Archives
Dianne Strang, UK Researcher
Late John van Gelder
Gerald O'Dea and Rodney Jordan.

I have no doubt that there will be some names that do not appear above, for that I apologise most sincerely.

Chapter 1

Beginnings

A while back, I chanced upon Bruce (Mac) Mackenzie at work on his family history. Intrigued, I took it upon myself to investigate my own family tree.

What a surprise, convicts everywhere! I discovered that my family history goes back to the First and Second Fleet. After much work, I discovered that my forefather was known by several names. This was mostly the case in those times, as education was almost an unknown quantity. His name was Samuel Pigott, Piggott, Pigote, Picket or Pickett.

He was sentenced to death at the Devon Assizes held in Exeter on the 20th March 1786 before Sir James Eyre, and Sir Beaumont Hotham, after being committed on 19th December for felony. The charge was:

'For feloniously cutting and stealing 2 pieces of woollen serge,

called druggett, containing 50 yards, value 40s: The goods of George Hayman in the racks in the night.'

Royal mercy was extended on condition of transportation for 7 years and so Samuel Piggott spent time at Plymouth on the hulk *Dunkirk*, before being transferred on March 11th 1787 to the *Charlotte*, one of the ships of the First Fleet. After only 8 months in the colony, he was transferred by the *Golden Grove* to Norfolk Island where he was put in charge of some gardens. Three months later he was put in irons and dispossessed of his garden for acting as a ringleader in a convict plot to take over the Island, only to be forgiven the following month for his 'useful activity' during a hurricane which swept Norfolk Island. It seemed that he could not stay out of trouble though as 4 years later, Samuel was again transported, this time by the *Atlantic*, and arrived in Sydney Cove on 30th September 1792 for trial for robbing the Government granary. Two years later he settled at Hawkesbury.

Mary Thompson arrived on the *Neptune*, a Second Fleet ship, on the 28th June 1790. She had been convicted at Lincoln on the 19th March 1789 for the theft of a silver watch, and in 1790 was on the convict muster for Norfolk Island. In 1791, she and Samuel Pickett were both issued with a pig, and later that year, in July they were both working a small piece of land together. Mary was also on the *Atlantic* back to Sydney on 30th September 1792. They had 4 children in the 1790s. The register at St. Phillips, Sydney, records the baptism in January 1796 of Ann Pickett, born 13[Th] September 1794 at

Hawkesbury. She was recorded as the daughter of Samuel and Mary Pickett, although I have found no records of Samuel Piggott and Mary Thompson's marriage in NSW. Who knows, they may well have been married on Norfolk Island, however a lot of the records for that time have been lost so this would be hard to follow up.

By 1806 they had twenty-five acres under crop and a family of 7 children: Ann, 1794, Mary 1797, Elizabeth 1799, Jane 1800, Charlotte 1803, Lucy 1804 and Dorothy 1806. Mary Pickett, at the age of 15 or so, married John Merrell/Murrell (convict) on the 31st May 1813 and they had 2 children, Ann and Bridgett.

Mary and John Murrell moved to Van Dieman's Land on board the brig *Sophia* in 1818 and settled in the Huon area, however sadly, Mary died aged 21 on 20th April 1819 in Hobart. Their daughter Ann married John Browning on 1st September 1830 in New Norfolk and they had 3 children: James, Henry and Mary Anne Millicent. Sometime between 1836 and 1837 this marriage broke up and Mary lived with George Labaun/Laburn, also an ex-convict, but he had received a conditional pardon in 1836. There were 2 more children from this relationship, however George obviously found it hard having a family as he was convicted of stealing a steer and sent to Port Arthur for 3 years.

Ann's next relationship was with William Clark(e) and she had more children with him, one of whom was my great grandfather, Charles Clark Browning, however they all have a variety of surnames. Some were Clarke, others Browning!

We know that William was born about 1813, but where and exactly when we have been unable to find out. There have been many family historians searching for many years but we have yet to definitely find his birth parents, or for that matter any lead that would help. Just one of those brick walls that sometimes are never scaled and here is the twist: my present day surname is Browning, but I have no Browning blood at all!

My Family Tree:

Samuel Pickett m Mary Thompson
= Mary Pickett b. 1797

Mary Pickett m John Merrill (Murrell)
= Ann Murrell b.

Ann Murrell m John Browning,
then George Laburn, then William Clark(e)
= Charles Clarke Browning b. 1848

Charles Browning m Eliza Ann Vernon Stretton
= Henry Browning

Henry Browning m Mabel Amelia Millyford Clayton
= Richard

Richard Browning m Elvie Adelaide Coleman   = Avelon Richard Browning b. 1941.

Chapter 2

Early Years

Faye, Darrel, Joan, Valerie, Anthony and myself 1945.

Life began for me on the 22nd January, 1941 at the Cottage Hospital New Norfolk Tasmania, the first son of Richard and Elvie Browning of Fentonbury, a small country town in the upper Derwent Valley. I was to be named Adrian Richard Browning but christened Avelon Richard Browning some 5 days later. It became apparent many years later, that there were 2 boys born on the same day, and as a result of an administrative mix-up, I ended up with the Christian name Avelon, instead of Adrian.

1941 was a time of world conflict with war raging in Europe and Asia and with rationing fully in place, it was very difficult to feed and clothe a family. Dad, with his father, was trying to farm vegetables and run some sheep and cattle on about one hundred acres, most of which was still heavily timbered. Our home livestock consisted of a milking cow, a few fowls and sometimes a pig to kill for the table. Add to this a couple of draught horses and that was it. Animal skins like wallaby and possum were in demand back then, but the hunting season was very short. As you may imagine quite a great deal of poaching took place — money was in very short supply and without the wallaby and rabbit to supplement our menu (and their skins to supplement the pocket), I'm sure we would have gone without food many times during my early life. Being the first son in the family didn't mean that I got any preferential treatment in any way either. Clothes were still handed down, in my case with some modifications — I had 3 older sisters! Two brothers were born after me then another sister. It was a busy house.

Butchering our own meat was the norm, however on some occasions, killing a beast was not as easy as it should have been. I recall one occasion when Dad and my grandfather were killing a steer. Dad had shot it with a .22 rifle and they then cut its throat. Both men were standing alongside the body sharpening their knives when all of a sudden it got up on all 4 legs, put its long horns through the 10 foot wooden gate and tossed it in the air! It ran for about 50 to 100 yards before stopping dead, and then died on its feet! A very drama-filled few seconds. I was only probably 5 or 6 years old when I hung off the fence watching it all; it was talked about for months.

The early years before school are somewhat sketchy but I do remember that even at that early age I was expected to put my shoulder to the wheel with the various tasks around the house. I recall clearly that all of us at some stage in our early years learnt how to set traps for rabbits. Back then conservation was not the issue it is today, if something else was trapped, then it was too bad – maybe even useful. Being able to harness the 2 draught horses ready for work was something we learnt as well. Being on the short side, it was always difficult for me to harness the horses. It must have looked funny; there was me standing on a box or hanging off the fence trying to get the tack over her head all the time hoping Dolly would not move! The other job we had was to give the stables a good muck out and give each horse their feed of chaff during the winter months.

I started school early in 1946, at the age of 5. It was the biggest step on life's road that I would take for some time and it was a very rough one. None of us could read or write, except for maybe our name, before we started school. The walk from home was about a mile through the bush, then on a dirt road for another 1/2 a mile or so to the bus stop, but to walk that last 500 yards was a very daunting task. There were kids from various families nearby that attended the same school, and for some time, our family were subject to verbal and physical abuse. The other kids would throw rocks at us to try and stop us getting on the bus. It was only the intervention of the bus driver that put a permanent stop to it. At school it was not much different. It wasn't the best way to make a start to school. I have no grudges towards them though, life is too short for that. Besides, I recently found out that we have something very special in common, family history and the same link to the First and Second Fleet – they were nearly all related to me in some way.

Learning at school was also something I found neither easy nor important. When I was 6, money was scarce and we went blackberry picking, the whole family. All of us camped in 2 tents for a few months. It was an experience I won't forget. We also had to change schools during that time. I can remember all of us children being rowed across the river each morning to walk to catch the school bus. It was about this time that Dad and my grandfather were hawking (selling) fruit and vegetables around several of the local townships to make ends meet. Quite often I would wag school to help Dad out when my grandfather was unable to make it. This would happen at least 2 days a week and on reflection it's no wonder my education standard never reached the heights it should have done. It wasn't always hard work though. Being adventurous, as most young ones are, we knew of an apple tree some miles away on the next door neighbour's property and we would go to great lengths to cover that ground without being seen. We would crawl through every deviation on the ground and the funny part about it was that the bloody apples were old seedlings, not worth the time of day, let alone the extra effort we would put into it each year to get them! It was a great adventure though and I suppose kids are still doing similar things these days.

Then there is the other incident during my primary school days that haunts me (and probably many others), the visit by the school dentist. We had a lady dentist. The fear of just sitting in the chair and worse, having a tooth pulled … well as they say, the first impression is the best or in this case the worst impression and it has stayed with me for 60 odd years!

So many things are different now. Having a daily shower was unheard of in my early years, we all lined up for the weekly baths on a Sunday night, what with water being a very scarce commodity. We had a concrete tank alongside the house for cooking and drinking and a tank catching the runoff from the barn for baths and the laundry which I may add was all done by hand. It took my mother and sisters all day to heat the copper and wash all the clothes, sheets etc. Then they all had to be wrung, dried and ironed!

Christmas, who can forget Christmas? The festive season did not rate anywhere near what we see today, but was still memorable. There was no media blitz. It was mainly a religious holiday, especially for the poorer people. Dad usually killed a pig, once a year, for our Christmas ham, if we were lucky. Many times I hung a sock at the end of the bed and woke up on Christmas morning to find it still empty, though I can recall once an uncle staying with us and he was given the task of building both my brother and I a wheelbarrow each for Christmas. I believe my parents had an ulterior motive as we were then able to get more wood and sticks in each day. It was a very sad day when Uncle Alf Smith passed away during his stay with us that year (1946). He was my grandmother's brother, a gentleman. Toys were an unknown item. I don't recall ever receiving a toy either for Christmas or for a birthday. I suppose one of the reasons was in those days there was never enough money to buy those types of items. We were influenced at an early age to make do with what was available around us. Today I have the means and the energy to seek and purchase many things that I like, however I still, as taught when I was young, only seek the things that are really needed. In a nutshell, the simple things in life are the ones that give me joy. Back then in the summer when the grass was dry, we found a piece of old roofing iron to use as a sledge and slid down the hill on it, or made little dams in creeks and big puddles in the winter. It was all part of learning some independence and enjoying life as we saw it. These are the joys of being young and not having a care in the world. The parents had to carry that responsibility.

Winter was very harsh at times. Frosts seem to be on the

ground every morning, some of it still there from the previous morning greeting me whilst doing the morning chores and again on the way to school. At times we would receive a heavy fall of snow, to the delight of us all as the snowfall gave everyone something different to have some fun with. To keep our hands warm during the cold frosty mornings, we would put a rock in the fire till it was nice and hot, then wrap it in newspaper and hold it.

Dad had a paddock of raspberries, probably a couple of acres as near as I can recall. There was no irrigation at all, what moisture was needed to promote their growth came out of the sky. Summer often had high humidity, with thunder storms frequent. When one considers the climate in that same area today, the raspberries would not survive for one day. My, how things have changed!

On the subject of 'climate change', there are many versions. My own view is simple: we, the human race, have taken planet Earth for granted for far too long. We have to turn it around. There are many natural contributions to climate change as in the recent volcano eruption in Brazil, but these are things beyond our control. Man-made pollution and misuse of the planet is in our control and should be addressed. Maybe if the politicians talked to us directly these days as they did when I was very young, things might be different. I can remember one that came out to the bush where we lived, walked half a mile up the dirt track just to talk to Dad to see if he had any concerns. They talked to as many people as they could. You wouldn't catch them door-knocking these days!

One time while visiting my grandparents, my Uncle Albert (Mick) Browning gave me his bicycle to keep. It was an old pushbike but I didn't mind at all because it gave me a means of getting about. I had great fun learning to ride it too! Our backyard was an acre of sloping land. I would get on the bike at the top and try to keep it upright until I got to the bottom. When I was successful doing that there was always the risk of flying over the net fence at the end! I was never badly hurt though, and would hop back on and try again. Uncle Mick was Dad's younger brother, a quiet unassuming man who I felt quite close to. So many times he took me fishing or shooting, yet he never spoke of his early life, some of which he spent in the Australian Army in Darwin during World War II.

I recall that I had my first brush with the law while riding that bike. Basil McCallum and I were riding our bikes from his place, on the wrong side of the road. Tom Jones was the local constable. Constable Jones had seen us earlier and just waited for us around a short bend, near the old church, put his hand up to stop us then chastised us very loudly, saying he would tell our parents. It scared us badly at the time, but thinking back now I don't recall hearing anymore about it. On one of his visits, Constable Tom Jones showed us a Luger pistol that he had (supposedly) taken off a German POW. He said that if he fired it at a small stump the gun was that good the bullet would pass through the stump. He even said he'd show us. Wasn't he embarrassed when it didn't come out the other side!

Bush fires were always a hazard during the summer months, so you can imagine our consternation when my brother and a cousin experimenting with having a smoke at the edge of one of the paddocks somehow managed to set the grass on fire. It took an hour or so of very hard work for us all to put that fire out! I can't remember what the punishment happened to be at the time, but there is no doubt there would have been some. Not that I was perfect. In my late teens, a friend and I would walk to the National Park Hotel to try to buy some beer. It was a long way to walk for a beer, I think we only did it twice and being underage and known in the community meant that we were not successful!

During our school holidays we were never idle. Pocket money was an unknown entity. Fruit picking was the order of the day and we, that is my younger brother and I, would leave home about 6:30 a.m., walk some 2 or 3 miles through the bush and pick either raspberries or blackcurrants for up to 10 hours a day. We'd get about 25 shillings a day. It seemed like a lot of money back then. These days that amount would only buy one eight-ounce beer! Then on the way home we'd spend about an hour swimming in the local dam. It was great fun for all of us. We would then walk home, do the chores and get ready for the next day. It was in that dam that I learnt to swim and when I went on to Glenora Area School, I passed my swimming test — all 15 yards dog paddle in the Styx River below the school. My swimming costume too was a hand-me-down from one of my sister's wardrobes — cut off at the waist! Another way we found to get a few extra bob was to travel the road with a sack bag each and collect bottles. We got about sixpence a dozen for beer bottles and about a shilling a dozen for cordial bottles — it all added up over a 12 month period. Then there was the bounty on blackbirds because of their pest status. I'm not sure how many we collected but they died very quickly with a .22 bullet.

We were encouraged to save even when there was little money about. Saving meant everything. During all my school days, money was always very scarce. The war and its after effects made things very tough for quite a few years. Having money and keeping it though is another thing. Between leaving school and enlisting, I invested in a business called Cox Brothers, a chain of clothing stores. It seemed like a good idea at the time, until they went broke and I lost the lot, about 1000 pounds I recall. A lot of money back then. Over the years I have seen many companies and investors come and go even in these days with constant screening from government bodies etc, and the bad ones continue to pop up. It shows that investors are still making mistakes — I don't feel so bad after all.

I got to meet a lot of the migrants that came out just after the war. I do recall that most only had the clothes that they came with, no money and a lot of perseverance, something that they had to have to survive. In the hydro villages, the winters were harsh with a lot of snow and frost. I met up with some of these people in later years after I came back home out of the Navy and one could see that they had worked very hard and so enjoyed a better life because of it.

It was about this time that we (my father and one of my brothers) bought a small fibreglass dingy and an outboard motor. We really thought we were pigs on a stick! We found some tank aerials to make the fishing rods out of. When time allowed we would head off to the lakes and try and catch some trout. There were not too many times we failed to bring home at least one good-sized trout. These are some of my best memories, going to one of the lakes, sometimes staying overnight just to try and catch that elusive trout: a lovely holiday for us all.

In the early part of 1951, I started at Glenora Area School in grade 6. It was probably the last year at school that I learned very much. It was a tough school. There were fights often and I can remember one between 2 of the kids. It was toe to toe with no quarter given by either, neither came out a winner. Then there was also the physical instructor that taught at the school who had a disagreement with one of those 2. He was taken into a nearby building and given a hiding, not the best advert for any school. There was not a day that would go past that we didn't get into trouble of some kind. I remember our teacher "Jesse James" (his last name was James so we nicknamed him Jesse). He was not a lot older than us at that time. About 4 or 5 years ago, I heard that he was still teaching!

In 1954, which was my last year of school (grade 9), our teacher was a Mr. Grey and I remember him as a gentleman. He had been a World War II Air Force pilot and during the day he would tell us stories of his time during the war and we all hung on his every word. There was one good thing about High School though. It was during that time all the boys had to take classes in sheetmetal work, leather work and carpentry. In grade 9 we also learnt blacksmithing. The late Tom Roberts was our blacksmith teacher at the time. It was something I excelled in and I represented the school at the Hobart show of 1954 with a great deal of pride. Sadly the call for the use of a blacksmith has slowly dwindled. His call in those times was strong, as there were a lot of farms and hops grown in that area. A lot of the work was done with draught horses.

The day approached that was to be my last day at school and at the time it couldn't get there quickly enough for me. Early November 1954 my exemption from attending school was given — my OK to leave school for the last time. The photo on the facing page is from that year as far as I can remember.

My first job was for Dad. He and I had a contract to put up 50 chains (just over 1000m) of fencing for a local landowner. The price agreed upon was 3 pound a chain. It was bloody hard work. Every part of it was done the hard way, not with ignorance, it was just the only way for the job to be done at the time. We had to carry on our backs all the wire, both plain and barbed along the fence line, all 50 chain of it and to get to the beginning of the fence line was another 50 chain, all up hill. We had to split all the fence posts by hand, as well as droppers, adjacent to the line and it was all iron-stone country. It took us 12 days to complete the job (which made it very good money in those days) and to this day, I use it as a benchmark for any other tasks that I undertake.

Back Row (left to right): Brian Brown, Robert Nichols, Barry Jenkins(?) Terry White(?), ?,

Standing (left to right):? ?, Ken Hickman, ? , Tony Marriott, Tony McCallum, Colin Glover(?),

Sitting (left to right):? Tas Browning, Durbin Cooper, ? , ?, Keith Clark, Brian McKenzie

Kneeling (left to right): ? Harris, Darrell McMaster, last 3

There were to be many other jobs that we undertook in those early years. One time we were employed to split fence posts, for the same land owner as before. We had to fell the trees and have them dragged out to the side of the road then cut them to length and split them. I recall quite vividly starting to fall the first tree by the light of a fire, my father on one side of the tree and myself on the other side. Both starting armed with axes, then using a cross cut saw in the back of the tree before the tree came down to earth — just as daylight broke! It all seems like yesterday. The landowner 'lent' us an old 2 man chainsaw for the sum of 2 pounds per hundred posts. That meant that we earned the sum of 8 pounds per hundred posts! The hardest part of the work was carrying those fence posts. They were green and being of peppermint gum, very close grained, making them much heavier. From memory they were 9 feet long so one can see how bloody heavy they were. There wasn't much of me in those days – I was only 15 or thereabouts, but it didn't take long for me to get fit.

It was at this time that all those with whom I went to school with, (some several years older), began to go their separate ways, some working away, some on farms and others enlisting in the services. By the time I was about 17 years old, the urge to move on beckoned me as well. There was always adverts in the newspapers for the Navy, Army and Air Force and in reality there was little for me at home with the farm barely able to sustain enough income for one and it was here the seed was sewn that would make big changes to my life forever.

Chapter 3

New Beginnings

> "You have been accepted into the Royal Australian Navy to train as a Naval Airman (non-flying) and are to report to the recruiting office at Franklin Wharf on the 22nd of February 1959 to be sworn in AM on the 23rd of February 1959."

In 1958, I decided to join the Navy. I set about getting the appropriate papers and spent days waiting for the mail each day in anticipation of being called up. It wasn't quite that easy though. As I lived some 40 odd miles from Hobart, I had to sit the exams, then have a medical and a session with the 'shrink'. As I recall, it all took about 2 days and during that time I had to stay at the YMCA. I failed my maths exam and was very upset about it; however the recruiting Chief Petty Officer was very good. He gave me some homework to do and pointed me in the right direction and as history shows I got through the next time.

It was during this period that the 'Konrad Kids' were in Hobart training and doing all those things that world class swimmers do to break records and while I was in Hobart I made a point of going to the pool and watching them swim. I was very impressed. In those days they were the best in the world. It made me want even more to be a part of the wider world, to see, feel and have my own adventures in it. When you set out on these life changes you don't realise that the adventure that you are about to embark on will make dramatic changes to your life, some of which are irreversible. I will say though that the friendships that came my way are still as strong as ever. I quite often remember my time in the Navy — everything I learnt and the mates I made, and kept — as the best years of my life.

Early February 1959, the mail arrived that I had been waiting for, it had seemed to take forever but I was in the Navy!

Having arrived in Hobart on the 22nd of February, I met 3 others that had made it through the process. They were Edward J Dell, James Eagles and Barry N Newman. We were sworn in the next day in a fairly simple ceremony. Finally we were in the Navy after what had seemed a very long time. The commitment we made was to defend Queen and country, something that our forebears had done in years past and some of them had paid the ultimate price. We had to celebrate so we went to the nearest pub, although we were all underage (the age to enter pubs was at that time 21). Before the hour was up we were asked to leave 3 pubs, with us arguing very loudly that we were in the Navy even though we hadn't got our uniforms yet!

Sadly Barry Newman did not stay the full term. My understanding is at one stage he chose to go AWOL and served 3 terms in Holdsworthy Military Prison before being discharged. Jim Eagles stayed in and did more than the initial term of 9 years. I have no idea of what became of Ted Dell as I have never come across him anywhere after our initial training.

The next day we were on a flight to Melbourne, a long flight in those days but it was a pretty good one to the big smoke. This was my first time out of Tassie, the first of many more both while I wore a uniform and during my later working life. We arrived at Essendon Airport early in the afternoon and there was a gathering from other states of recruits heading in the same direction as we were. We were bussed to the railway station and arrived at *HMAS Cerberus* early in the afternoon.

I was quite astounded by the enormity of the place and the people who were within its area. We were marched to the main stores to be issued with our bedding, together with a hammock, something I had never seen before, let alone slept in. Mind you, after training I never had the opportunity to use a hammock at sea as we had bunks on *HMAS Melbourne* as well as the various shore establishments I was to serve in. Our dormitory (D Block) was huge, with pipe rails going in all directions set in place to sling the hammocks. Probably about 100 blokes were together in each dormitory, but I don't recall how many dormitories there were. What did strike me was that for the previous 18 years having a bath had been a very private affair, while here in the Navy it was a very public part of the ablutions every day. When I was on board *Melbourne*, because fresh water was always at a premium, while one person wet their body under the shower, another was soaping then took his turn to shower down; being 'au natural' was unnoticed.

There seemed to be a lot of clothing issued to each of us but as we were to soon find out, each piece had its own role to play. Then we were marched to our accommodation that would house us for some 6 months or thereabouts. We were shown several times how to sling our hammock and stow it in its proper place and there were many of us that took quite a long time to get it right. There was a fair bit of fun as well with men falling out, or being rolled out!

By this time we were allocated into our various divisions — ours was air division with Petty Officer (Paddy) Burke as our instructor for the duration. It was here that I would learn all about how to keep the uniform in top condition. Ironing the uniform was unusual as most of it was ironed inside out, which made it appear very dressy and smart. We learnt quickly how to keep our kit well, as right from the start we had to have our full kit out for inspection at any time on the command of any one of the training officers. Another part of our issue of clothing and equipment was anti-flash gear and a respirator. The anti-flash gear was made mostly of cotton and treated to take a certain amount of heat when worn and never to be washed — when they got too dirty we would source another set from stores. With all this to keep clean and neat, we were allocated only 3 small lockers each. Our civvies were sent home and it was then that reality finally began to set in. We were no longer our own person.

The 'indoctrination' began straight away. We were marched everywhere and may I say here that none of us really knew what we were about to experience.

The first 2 weeks were taken up with having medicals, injections and getting kitted out with all our clothing and the parade ground 'goodies'.

It was about this time we were introduced to the parade grounds. One was named the 'Bull Ring' for obvious reasons and the other's name was 'Gods Little Acre'. No one was allowed to walk across it. If you were caught, it was so many times that you had to go around it with the rifle and bayonet fixed and held at arm's length above your head until the instructor gave an instruction to the contrary. For our parade ground routine, when needed, we used the old, now obsolete .303 rifle with bayonet.

The whole discipline thing with everything having to be done at the same time, all people having to respond at the same time to someone else's seemingly random orders, was for me, my biggest learning curve at this time. I'm sure everyone else was in the same position as I was. Part of our training was with respirators. We had to test them in a chamber where tear gas was used. A group of us were ushered into the chamber with our gas masks on and told to take them off. None of us stayed there too long after that, we were out the door looking for fresh air.

In early March, I was not feeling too good and reported to the sick bay. After a quick check over I was shown a bed for the night. The doctor on duty next day diagnosed that I had left lobar pneumonia with low blood pressure of 90/60 which gave an added diagnosis of ventricular damage – myocarditis.

I was to spend some 37 days in hospital and for about half of those days I never knew where I was or for that matter, why. I do recall having many ECGs. They scrubbed the areas where the leads were to be attached to my chest with a very hard toothbrush — it was probably a good thing that I was half out of it.

During my long stay in hospital I began talking to a Seaman in the bed opposite me who asked me from which state I had come. I said Tasmania and it was he who set in place my nickname that is still with me to this day — 'Tas'. It was also during my stay in the hospital that I had the misfortune to have a bloke dumped in a bed opposite me. He had hardly any skin left on his head – he was a mess! I found out he had been caught stealing many things from fellow recruits and the no skin bit was as a result of him 'falling down the stairs'. From memory, he was sentenced to 90 days in Holsworthy Military Prison and discharged.

The funny thing about my illness was that the Senior Medical Officer sent a letter to my mother referring to my time in hospital, telling her I had a slight touch of bronchitis. After I was released I was given a further 3-week sick leave to recover, not bad but they did not at any time explain to me what my health problem actually was. It would be many years before I would find all those details out.

Those 3 weeks went very slowly. I made sure of that. When I returned back to camp the faces had all changed. The crew I had started with had all finished their training and those that were headed to Nowra had gone. It was a 'stop-and-start' go for me. Because the class that was going through had just started training, I had to be the office runner for another 6 weeks so that I could pick up when the new class reached the same point as when I left the old class.

Again Paddy Bourke was our training Petty Officer and I have to say he did his job well. It was during our initial training here at FND (Flinders Naval Depot) that we were taken out onto the rifle range. We were given Bren guns, Thompson machine guns and a mortar and taught how to handle and fire them effectively.

'The Millionaires Club' was in effect a cafe that served us well, as we were not allowed into the wet mess during training. It was here that we all took to the milkshakes that were sold and I for one soon put on a bit of weight. Not that we didn't work it off during our training but when all was said and done we were only young blokes and still growing. Training continued at a fairly fast pace. We were indoctrinated well, very well, as even to this day I can recall with no hesitation, my official number and information that was drilled into us. Though some may not see it in the same light, I thought the process helped bring most of us closer together. After our initial period of training we were allowed to have a short leave. We all headed into Melbourne, and it was here that I met a young girl who, as I recall, was a Richmond supporter. They were playing Geelong on that day and I've been a Geelong supporter ever since. Unfortunately the romance did not continue, but I think it was my moving to Nowra that cut it short.

On the 3rd July 1959, we all got our first mid-winter official leave. Rex Cox, Ian Howard, Rex Cook and I took the train from Flinders Naval Depot (*HMAS Cerberus*). By the time we arrived at the Frankston Railway Station it was decided that the train was too slow, so off we got and we took a taxi into the city leaving our gear at the airline terminal before marching into the nearest pub. I would have to add I was the new boy on the block as far as going into a pub and bending the elbow like these blokes were doing, but I tried! Needless to say, I was definitely the worst for wear the next morning.

One of the tasks that we all had to learn pretty quickly was the art of washing our clothes. Electric washing machines were a rare thing at shore establishments and even much rarer on ship. We got around that by a simple 'invention' called a 'Pogo Stick'. It was made of copper. A 6-inch funnel, upside down with a 2ft 6-inch pipe welded onto it with a cross piece of copper pipe welded to that. We must not forget the remainder of the tools needed either: a 4-gallon bucket. Were you to possess this collection of items you were often in great demand!

By the time August had come around we had almost finished our training. The day before we were drafted to Nowra (on board *HMAS Albatross*) we had the big march past, all of us in our best-dressed uniform. We left Cerberus on the 19th of August for the train trip north and it was a trip that I would have trouble forgetting. Sitting in what could be best described as dog boxes, I'm sure that no one got any sleep at all that night. I do recall that the train stopped at Albury for a change over which was for about an hour and everyone headed for the bar on the station. We got into Central Station in Sydney mid-morning the next day feeling very tired and a bit rough and headed to another platform to catch the train to Bomaderry Station (Nowra), arriving there about midday. *HMAS Albatross* was also a big culture shock for us all, a lot of noise, what seemed to be a lot of aircraft flying in all random directions. Confusing, but we would discover everything was done with precision. It was back to reality for us. After doing our draft-in procedures we were guided back to the classroom — this time to learn the fundamentals of each area of the Fleet Air Arm which is very wide-ranging.

Ordinance, engines, airframes, meteorology, the list goes on. It was a pretty hectic 12 weeks to say the least, from one classroom to another and of course not forgetting the parade ground time as well. It was on the 18th. October 1959, that we were all drafted to *HMAS Penguin* (near Sydney) to do a damage control course which was very intense but only because it had to be. We had to basically learn how to save the ship in many scenarios as well as saving ourselves. It all took about 14 days and then it was back to Nowra.

At long last the selections were made as to who would do what course, where and when. I was selected to do the Aircraft Handlers course which took some 8 to 12 weeks and during this period we were taught all aircraft handling procedures both at sea and ashore as well as firefighting techniques both at sea and ashore. Part of the firefighting tuition was to put out a fire in an old aircraft as well as rescue 2 dummies in the aircraft. I was selected as number 2 rescuer for this exercise, and everything proceeded as planned. After handing over the rescued dummy I found it very hot with all the protective gear I had to wear. This was because it was an asbestos treated firefighting suit with fire safety boots. I had no vision at all as perspiration had fogged up the visor of my helmet, so I took off my helmet. In doing so I copped a face full of foam. It tasted bloody terrible and the smell was just as bad, but we had done an excellent job and saved the 2 dummies and received good marks for the exercise.

We all passed out with some glee and the best thing was that now we were allowed into the wet canteen for a beer. It was here that each branch of the Fleet Air Arm had their own table to sit at and the 'handlers' were no exception. We were called the 'Ralphs' and as I recall to be able to sit at that table one had to first be initiated. To pass this initiation you had to, in one hour, consume 10 x 10oz beers. Sounds simple doesn't it? You had to sit down in the one spot, walk to the bar, buy your beer, and sit back down at the table before you could consume your beer. Repeat this 10 times within the hour. Let me tell you it's lucky I only had to do it once, never again!

I can also recall meeting a young lass on my mid-winter leave while I was visiting my sister. We both agreed to write to each other and basically left it at that. I went back to Nowra and not long after I received a letter from her mother, telling me that she did not agree to my relationship with her daughter Doreen and stating that we should not see each other again. I was only 20 at the time and the lass was several years younger than I, so our age made it complicated. I wrote back to her mother and set out my feelings on the matter. It was on my next leave that I visited my sister again and met the parents and I must say they were very good to me and treated me like a son, but as it turned out the relationship did not play a very big role in our lives. I had by then witnessed too many of the blokes that I had joined up with ending up with broken marriages. Not for me. Our relationship was never that good and it went through the stages of gradually falling apart and that was it.

We would now be allocated to various positions around the air station and I was sent to help out with duties in the Chief Petty Officers' mess while we all waited for notice of our first postings to *HMAS Melbourne*. It was not long for us to wait, as we were to join *HMAS Melbourne* on the 10th of October 1960. I think we were all packed up and ready to go several days before the big day – I know I was. Another train and bus trip and we reached our first posting. Our first impressions were of disbelief and dismay, we'd been told the size but to see it in the raw was awesome. How would we find our way around? If we thought it was big we were in for a bigger shock. It wasn't long before we got a look at the American aircraft carriers that were operating in South East Asia. They were even bigger! We made our way onto the ship and proceeded to start our draft in. This procedure lets each department know of our arrival on the ship. I was billeted in 2 November mess deck, which is situated just below flight deck level, and just aft of the Island structure. I tagged onto both Ron Jesse and the late Keith (Baron) Kettley for several days as it was just a maze of hatches and passageways.

After all the fuss of the first day we unpacked our gear and would you believe it, our lockers were down in the 7 Kilo section! That was 6 decks below where we slept. We had no kit lockers in our mess deck either. Our everyday items we somehow stored in our bunk area. It was during my stay in 2 November mess deck that I had my wallet stolen with my pay in it. With everyone living so close together in the mess, how could you possibly know who took it and why? At the end of 1961, I had to throw away everything I had stored in my locker. It was as if it had all been cooked! All dried up, cracked and rotten they were. It was that bloody hot down there — being alongside the engine room. Then there were the sleeping arrangements. The bunks were small in size with just enough room to lay flat and the mattress, on reflection, only one to 2 inches thick. Conditions were pretty cramped and the bunks were sometimes 5 bunks high. However for those of us that served, you had to accept the conditions: regimented, basic, sometimes harsh but with a lot of comradeship and fellow feeling. It also made you really appreciate going home on leave. Then a soft bed was one of the things I always looked forward to.

We met our Flight Deck Officer Lt. CDR (Shady) Lane and the Flight Deck Chief Jack (Sparrow) Finch who both would endear themselves to all concerned. The Captain would be Captain V.A.T. Smith, a man that set new standards with flight deck routines as well as aircraft movements both on and off the flight deck. He was the founding father of the Fleet Air Arm. In the weeks that followed we learnt all the various routines that make the flight deck tick and also about the ship in general. It was during this time I received a telegram from my father, saying that my grandfather (his dad) had passed away.

He had been a special person to me. He had it very tough

in his lifetime but never complained. A sad time, but life went on and the busy routine-filled days helped. While we were training, the ship remained alongside the fitting out wharf undergoing its annual refit. Being a part of *HMAS Melbourne's* Ship's Company was in itself an education for us first timers, and there were other initiations into Navy life that we were yet to be shown in the coming days. This entailed a trip ashore to the 'Rockers', the proper name for those uninitiated is the Macquarie Hotel. It always took place on a pay night. The event was the raffle, a common event, the raffling of one of the 'girls'. It was a frequent part of the pubs events and no, I did not win any of them! There would be women fighting (as well as men) and some would be at it toe to toe; it was a pretty rough place. From there, after the pub closed, would be a stopover at Harry de Wheels for a pie and peas and quite often there would be a floor show of some kind somewhere else during the evening.

Early in November the ship was moved to the inner Captain Cook Dock, this being the dry dock and we would spend the rest of the month there. We were sent on our annual leave on the 10th of December with 17 whole days to soak up the local life at home because we had 6 months of sea time ahead of us. As soon as we arrived back onboard the *Melbourne*, we were all put to work loading stores onto the ship. I have to say on reflection that it was pretty hard work though we were mostly young and fit so we didn't feel too much pain, and there were some benefits. One job was loading the beer on board. It was stored down on 7 Deck and it took all day. We lost quite a deal of sweat so we helped ourselves to the occasional can or bottle of beer. They were not very cold but they went down well! Early in January 1961, the ship moved to Number 3 Buoy to load ammo and aviation fuel, the ship's Captain was changed on the 8th of January with Captain V.A.T. Smith DSC RAN taking command of *HMAS Melbourne* and we were finally ready to leave.

Harry de Wheels van.

At 9:30 a.m. on the 11th of January, *Melbourne* cast off from the fitting-out wharf, my first taste of going to sea! During the coming weeks we would undergo a lot of training as most of the flight deck crew were new to the task.

HMAS Queenborough was our ship in company and she would act as our sea/air rescue ship during flying operational work and training. Our ship's divers would undergo their training programs as well. Diving at night was something special to see. We were in and out of Jervis Bay frequently as that was where the Naval College was situated for the training of Naval Officers before arriving back in Sydney, only to leave again on the 31st in company with a Kiwi ship *HMNZS Royalist*. In the afternoon both squadrons embarked their aircraft. Seeing so many aircraft landing on during such a short time frame for the first time was something to see, but one I grew used to. We left with 2 scientists from the CSIRO. They joined the ship for a fortnight and their task was to determine the proportion of the sun's energy that is reflected by the sea.

There was a shuffle of manpower and I was moved to hangar duties. Here I joined Bob Gilmore, Pat Franklin, Harry Jenkins, Ace Klieden, Trevor Chatterton and a few others whose names I cannot recall. Bill Gardner was the Hangar Chief with Knobby Hall the Hangar Officer.

Probably one bonus of serving in *HMAS Melbourne*, (if there was such a bonus), was the beer issue. It cost about one shilling and 3 pence for a 26oz can of VB and cigarettes were about 9 pence for a pack of 20. Both items were duty free. Another bonus was the dress code: a pair of shorts and sandals! This was a big help in the tropics.

HMAS Melbourne passed through Port Jackson Heads at 0445Hrs on the 3rd February, and at 0500hrs the ship commenced DG Ranging off Shark Point. Because of the limited turning room at the end of each run, 2 tugs were employed to assist with the turns. On one occasion Operation Pin Wheel was used. This employed 3 Venom aircraft forward and aft on one side. They would start up their engines and the thrust would push the ship round. The rate of turn was far quicker than tugs, albeit much noisier. Degaussing was completed at 1020 hrs. after 12 runs over the range. (This was done for protection against mines and other means of intrusion.) Perhaps here I should give an outline of the aircraft hangars that we all would spend many hours in. There are 3 hangars A, B and C, A being the biggest then B then C. To enter them one has to go through an airlock at that deck level, with the only other entries being the forward and aft aircraft lifts from the flight deck. Each of these hangars is separated by a fire curtain, which is impregnated with asbestos. In this environment it gets extremely hot creating high levels of fire risk. The flow of fresh air was always very limited, as the aircraft lifts were sometimes lowered only whilst no flying aircraft was close to the ship.

After a few days of work up, the ship headed towards the city of Melbourne in company with the *Queenborough* and *HMS Royalist* and on the 9th of February we tied the ship up to Station Pier. During our stay in Melbourne there would be a family day for those Victorian crew members. About 15,000 people visited the ship. *HMAS Melbourne* left Melbourne on the 13th of February for passage to Fremantle, WA. It was during the voyage to WA that we would work very hard, finetuning the crew and machinery to their best work rates. There was a wharf strike on when the ship arrived in

Fremantle but we managed. During the day, fuel, oil, Avcat and Avgas were embarked. The ship was opened for visitors again and about 11,000 people visited the ship. On the 20th *Melbourne* sailed out for family day with good weather being in our favour. It was a lovely day, but unfortunately the ship could not return to the wharf to offload the guests. The strike was stopping us berth! The problem was solved by transferring the passengers to *HMAS Queenborough* and then taking them ashore on other boats.

It was compulsory to attend church services on the ship if one was on board, so on the last Sunday of our time in Perth, my mate and I chose instead to have a look around the city. We had 10 shillings between us when we went down the gangway and were met by a young couple with 2 children. They ushered us into their car and took us around the city area and to Kings Park. It was there that they opened up the boot and out came the picnic gear with a couple of bottles of beer. It was mid-afternoon when they took us back to the ship and even offered us money. We declined the offer of course, but it left a lasting impression of the kindness of the people of Perth! Normality returned, and we set off this time leaving Australian waters.

Chapter 4.

South East Asia Here We Come.

It was during this trip to South East Asia that I learned to play cards. I thought that I knew something about cards until I saw the likes of some of the blokes that I served with — they knew the game inside out. It cost me a few bob on the way but the dividends did flow my way when the cards fell into place, so to speak, especially when me and a bloke by the name of 'Speed King' challenged anyone to a game of Bridge, so much a point, we had it down pat. As I recall we were never beaten.

It was with some small delays but the exercise got under way. The ship had been very hot between decks, especially when rough weather or darken ship precluded scuttles being open. Water rationing had to be introduced to combat the excessively high fresh water consumption. Mind you, the ship was limited in its making of fresh water, from memory about 500 tons every 24 hours which is not a lot of fresh water when you consider that there is about 1,200 men on the ship. The health and morale of the Ship's Company was very good, in fact, all the better for being able to spend a relatively long period, for peacetime, at sea.

The very large exercise that was taking place gave all of the crew very little time to eat, sleep and work and there was never much time to sleep when the ship was operational. My first time at sea was a very real experience, as on the 4th of March we would have our first experience of losing an aircraft at sea. There was no panic. It really shone out how everyone handled their individual jobs. That time we lost a Sycamore helicopter with people being transferred to *HMS Hermes* for discussion in regards to the exercise that was underway

On the 9th of March the exercise continued but sadly a Gannet aircraft and its pilot were lost during the forenoon from *HMS Hermes*. Even in so-called peace time there is always a high price that is paid, this time with the loss of a life. It was early on the 10th of March that *HMAS Melbourne* tied up to Buoy Number 4 Trincomalee, Ceylon (Sri Lanka now). We had come a long way from Sydney and this was, for most of the Ship's Company the first foreign port of call.

During our short stay here in Trincomalee, I do recall a member of the flight deck crew being arrested for alleged smuggling and theft of cigarettes. His sentence for that offence was, as I recall, 89 days detention. This was started in the cells on board and the remainder of his sentence was carried out in Changi in Singapore. I was one of a few that had my turn as cell sentry on this person. As it turned out he was one of the blokes that I had joined up with though he was from the Banana State (Queensland). One of the things the person in the cell at that time had to do was pick hemp. From what I can remember the hemp had to be of so much weight and it had to be un-picked from its rope stage to a heap of fluff. His fingers were not in a very good state when he had finished.

As I recall there were some 60 odd ships here in Trincomalee, the biggest fleet in that harbour since the Second World War. The heat and humidity were at a high level, which of course is expected in this part of the world. One change that became very evident was that here in the tropics when having a shower it was not necessary to use any hot water! The cold water line was warm enough in itself. Leave was given till 11 p.m. each day. During exercise Jet, *Melbourne's* 2 fixed wing squadrons flew some 160 sorties, with an average daily serviceability of 10 Sea Venom and 9 Gannet aircraft, not bad at all. The air crew of the Venom averaged 9hrs 45 min. and the Gannet aircrew averaged 17 hrs and 17 min. for the 8 days that they were required for the exercise. It was one of the experiences of a lifetime to see my first foreign country. The 4 days that we were in Trincomalee was the longest period that we had spent in a rest period since the 11th of January.

For my first time in a foreign port, it all seemed so strange to me, a culture shock to say the least. Not knowing any of their customs was the hard part, although many of them could speak very good English. During our brief stay many of the crew would swim over the side of the ship. Several of the duty crew would patrol the flight deck with the old .303 rifle just in case there were any sharks about. Life ashore from what I can recall was fairly basic, Trincomalee did not appear to be a big town and it's hard to remember just how big it was. Several of us made it ashore on the second day to have a look around and being sailors we visited the first pub, strictly for education purposes may I add. The pub had a dirt floor, tables and seats. We sat down and after some discussion decided that we would try their beer. Surprise, surprise! Out came the young man with the beer but each bottle was different as well as the labels! Needless to say we only tried the one and to top it off it cost 10 shillings: very expensive indeed.

The four-day stay moved on very quickly and the ship moved out of harbour at 8 a.m. on the 14th of March heading for Bombay in India. The ship continued with flying exercise. This kept the aircrew up to scratch. Mind you, my opinion of the aircrew has always been that they are among the best if not the best. One has to only see these aircraft land on and take off to see what the aircrews are made of. On the final approach of these aircraft and looking forward from the cockpit the flight deck must look so small compared to a normal airstrip, but they have done it so many times. They are, to coin an old phrase, 'magnificent men in those flying machines'. We entered Bombay Harbour on the 18th of March at 9 a.m.

Bombay was a city with laws that regards alcohol with some disdain. A few of us decided to make the move and go ashore to have a good look around. Having prohibition in place here placed an obstacle in the way of having a social drink. We found our way to their version of a NAAFI club, which by the South East Asian standards was pretty darn small, and an education to say the least. Beer was in what we used to know as 26oz bottles in wooden crates, these were tipped into a bath with brown ice and in a matter of about 5 minutes a bottle was pulled out, then opened and poured into a long glass with some of that brown ice. I soon changed my drink to a nip of whisky. Unfortunately that got a similar treatment as the beer. There is another part of Bombay that is still very vivid in my mind. After leaving the NAAFI club we decided to take a dray ride around a few of the streets. We visited the 'Street of Cages'. The buildings on either side of the street were several stories high and the street was, from memory, some half a mile long. The rooms in these buildings were in actual fact brothels. Not one of us paid a visit! The women in these brothels were said to be of every nationality, hard to believe. Many of these women were out on their balconies trying to entice us to visit, not the done thing for sure. Poverty was rife in Bombay. I recall seeing a young woman with some 6 or 7 younger children all poorly dressed begging for food and to make even more of an impact on me she was pregnant. People lived and died on the street.

You could actually buy beer from a hotel in Bombay, but you had to make a declaration to the effect of your need for the drink and it must be consumed in 24hrs! We didn't stay too long in Bombay, leaving on the 20th of March for Karachi in Pakistan. We arrived there on the 22nd of March with the weather not giving us the best invitation to town. Here the ship anchored out some 2 miles from the breakwater. Sadly the weather prevented us from going ashore during our short stay. In fact, one of the flight deck handlers was one of the ship's boat crew and as a consequence of the rough weather that prevailed during our stay, he was injured and was hospitalised in Karachi and medevaced home.

On the 23rd of March the ship dressed overall for Pakistan Day. It was the next day that the ship sailed again, this time heading for Singapore. We continued to be kept very busy with flying operations every day. We still had *HMAS Queenborough* as our escort who also operated as our sea and air rescue ship during flying operations. A radar landfall was made on Great Nicobar early on the 31st. Some maintenance had been underway in the engine room to stop steam leaks and to reduce water consumption by the engines thus abolishing water rationing. Handy for us crew while we were in the tropics! On the 1st of April, *Melbourne* in company with *HMAS Queenborough* steamed eastward across the northern entrance of the Strait of Malacca towards Penang to collect mail from a Royal Navy ship. The ship dropped anchor some 25 miles east of Horsburgh lighthouse and because we were well ahead of the time to be alongside in Singapore, we were tasked to clean and paint the ship. At 0630 hrs on the 4th 8 Gannet and 10 Venom aircraft were flown off to Seletar Airfield and took part in the Singapore International Air Show which took place during our stay. After the fly off the ship we berthed in the Singapore Naval dockyard and tied up. We stayed in Singapore for some 8 days.

When I was first posted to *Melbourne* I had set a goal to buy as many 'Rabbits' (duty free goods) as my money would allow. I had brought an extra 150 pounds with me to buy all this stuff and here I was at the first port of call that was duty free, Singapore. There was no doubt about it there was plenty to spend one's money on here in Singapore, but considering the 3 previous ports that we had called at really didn't have anything that resembled night-life I hardly bought anything!

One of the most humorous 'events' that took place during our stay in Singapore was a competition between several of our flight deck crew. The competition was to see who could get the most tattoos on their 'appendage', the last count was 50 — I'm not sure if it was Greasy Howard or Geoff, who came out the winner. The late Warren Donahue whom I had gone to school with was also on *Melbourne*, and prior to arriving here we both had made a loose pact that when we got to Singapore we would get a tattoo. During our stay in Singapore the ship had a summer routine, starting work early and finishing early, mainly because of the heat and humidity. We both stepped ashore in the early afternoon on the first day and got a Mercedes taxi into the city and went to the NAFFI club to quench our thirst. From there we headed to the nearest tattoo parlour. I had a couple of swallows etc. tattooed on my left arm, not very big at all.

Warren had 2 nude women tattooed on the front of his thighs! I might add here that we were both wearing white shorts and tee shirts so both tattoos showed up pretty well. We went and had a few more beers and because of our dress code had to be back at the ship before sundown. As we went up the gangplank, the Officer of the Watch was on duty and took one look at the tattoos on Warren's legs and ordered him back in to Singapore to have some clothes put on the naked bodies on his legs. We both had a lot of laughs about it for quite some time after.

During our stay here curfew was, from memory, 11 p.m. each day because of the ethnic and political unrest. Another part of the 'education' of being in South East Asia was to visit the wet messes there. The Poms would clean up the left-over beer, be it in a glass or on the tables. They had buckets and virtually put in all the dregs they could find then would take them back to their messes and drink it! Yuck!

Singapore was at this time a very untidy place, poverty was rife and just about anything goes. The place to visit was 'Boogie Street'. Early in the evening the street was blocked off and tables and chairs came out alongside the various coffee stalls, little bars and other buildings. What did take a little while to work out were the Benny Boys. These were men dressed as women who were prostitutes into the bargain. We learnt a lot, that's for sure. The time went very quickly for us.

We left Singapore on the 13th of April to take part in

another exercise Pony Express, the 1961 SEATO naval exercise. During this exercise the force were making their way to Manila. At 1230 on the 16th a transfer of personnel was conducted to *Melbourne* from ships that were in company to take part in an athletic afternoon on the flight deck. The results of the day were *Melbourne* 1st, *The Voyager* 2nd and the *Marines* 3rd. At dawn on the 17th the mountains near Subic Bay were sighted and at 0630 *Melbourne* started refuelling ships of the force. On completion of this task *Melbourne* proceeded to Subic Bay berthing at Leyte Wharf at the Naval Air Station Cubi Point. During one of our short stays here there was a trip organised to visit Corregidor Island. We were taken there in a landing craft supplied by the Americans. It was an awesome place; a truck took us to the tunnel entrance. It had been an underground army camp during the Second World War. In fact, General MacArthur had his HQ there. The gun emplacements were huge. The tunnels were very big, one could drive a bus through them with ease. It was said that when MacArthur came back to the Philippines and took the island back off the Japanese, they filled the tunnels with dead Japanese.

The next day *Melbourne* went back to sea for a bit of a show day, returning in the afternoon to its berth. We were given a really great welcome, and visited the various clubs on the base. We sailed again early on the 19th with all the Australian ships meeting for independent exercises and returning to Manila Harbour late that same day. We stayed there this time for 2 days giving some of us a bit of shore leave in what we were told was a pretty wild city at the best of times. The Yellow Bar had the reputation as the place to visit and have your back to the wall so to speak. During our stay curfew was at 11 p.m. each day but the problem with that was we would get back to the landing where the liberty boats would pick us up, and it would take another 2 or more hours after that to get back to the ship! One time we were waiting at the landing after a hard day's night along with several thousand others and I recall one of our number was well under the weather. With a quick flick of the wrist he took a pistol from the holster of a Filipino policeman and started to wave it around. Another policeman placed a pistol in his back and gave the order to 'Give it up or else' (or words to that effect). It could have meant a sticky end but common sense prevailed, the crewman never went back ashore during the remainder of our stay in Manila. My greatest memory of Manila was the amount of guns that nearly everyone carried. Life did not carry a great deal of value in that part of the world.

One would quite often see gangs riding around on motorcycles armed to the teeth. Then we were back at sea and full-on with exercise Pony Express. This was designed as an amphibious operation with a landing of ground forces on the beaches of North Borneo. We left Manila for the last time on the 22nd carrying out anti-submarine exercises. On the 28th rehearsal landings were carried out at Balambangan Island and while these were in progress *Melbourne* was some thirty miles out at sea patrolling the area with the other screen ships. Sport was a priority within the ship's social structure but in an aircraft carrier like the *Melbourne* space is always in demand and very hard to come by, in the main because of aircraft movements, both in the air and within the ship. However over 300 of the Ship's Company played in volleyball competitions and 150 played deck hockey and 6 passed their provisional swimming tests.

It was during this time, while I was on my first trip out of Australian waters that Tasmania experienced high floods. The Derwent Valley that year (1960) recorded the biggest floods on record so far — with flood waters covering the hop grounds in the Bushy Park and close by areas. My father played a role in that flood by rescuing people from the Rum Jungle area along with many other people. Some of these people were to receive decorations for their brave work, others, like my father, received a letter of praise from the Police Department as they risked their life also. My parents never said anything about all this and I did not find out until after my mother passed away in 2009 and I found it in their papers.

On completion of exercise Pony Express off the coast of North Borneo, *Melbourne* made a heading for Hong Kong, refuelling on the way from RFA Wave Master. The Waglan Lighthouse was raised at 0450hrs on the 8th of May at 0645, 6 Sea Venoms and 2 Gannets were flown off to the RAF Station Kai Tak where they remained for the duration of our stay in Hong Kong. I had been waiting several years to get to this place and here I was, itching to get ashore. During our stay in Hong Kong they hired Chinese coolie labourers. This saved us a lot of work and I suppose was a lot cheaper as well. It was said of the Chinese labourers that they received about 10 shillings a day and if they lifted their heads during work, it was instant dismissal, with a line-up outside the gate waiting for a job. Our work routine here was similar to what we had in Singapore which was pretty hard to take! The ship was tied up in the dockyard at North Arm Naval Base so it was close to the China Fleet Club and anything that you wanted for that matter. The city of Hong Kong was filled with bars, not forgetting the girls that worked in them. There was even a bar called the Suzy Wong Bar — plenty to choose from! We were on duty one day in 4 so that gave us all plenty of shore leave. Plenty of bars lined the main areas, beer was cheap. Money played the main role in being able to get ashore. My 150 pounds that I had left Australia with was looking pretty sick at this point in time. Everyone was very busy on our first day in port, reading all our mail, as it was the first mail received since Manila.

On the 18th of May we were told that the ship might have to proceed to sea to get away from a typhoon that was heading our way. I was on duty watch that same day and I wanted to get ashore as I had big plans. I offered 5 pounds for anyone to do my duty for me, but alas I had no takers. About 5 p.m. the ship slipped away from the wharf and headed out to sea. We had left nearly half of the Ship's Company ashore as we had no time to wait for them. We were split into 2 duty watches and my first duty was in the hangar. We were issued with stretchers to sleep on, but had to lash them to the deck of the hangar just to sleep on them. We certainly had a wild ride while we were at sea. Typhoon 'Alice' passed over Hong Kong while we were out at sea and caused a little damage to the Island. The crew that had not made it back to the ship had made hay while they could and as I have been told, all did have a ball! My big plan had fallen over.

When we came back into Hong Kong we tied up to Number 1 Buoy which was only a short boat ride to either Hong Kong Island or to the Kowloon Mainland. When the ship first got to Hong Kong and we had tied up to the wharf, there was a group of Chinese women who came on board. I was to learn that their presence was for many purposes. One of these was to paint the sides of our ship, another was to collect the plates after each of our meals. All the leftovers from these plates were put into bins and they would take them to several orphanages. What we thought of as ordinary fare, was a feast to the orphans! One other role they took on was to sell goffas (cordial). The name of this group of women was Jenny's Side Party, of course led by Jenny. She was one special lady, who sadly passed away recently.

Hong Kong at that time was a fairly wild place. A few of our blokes decided to make some money while there with the game of Crown and Anchor. All forms of gambling were considered illegal in the Navy except for Tombola or Bingo, and then only if the funds raised went to charity. Those blokes spent as much time playing the game as they did checking to see if the Naval Police or the Red Caps would come in the door — hardly relaxing, but profitable for some!

On the 23rd of May the ship headed back to sea southeast to Manus Island for refuelling, then back to Sydney – home! On the 7th of June the ship passed through the Grafton Passage on its way to Townsville and that evening the Ship's Company was entertained by a concert in the hangars. There were many skits and variety acts to see and it was late that evening when the ship anchored in Cleveland Bay. At 6 a.m. north Queenslanders were transferred by boat to *HMAS Voyager* then on to Townsville, a quick stop in Moreton Bay to drop off more men, then on to Jervis Bay to disembark the squadrons of aircraft as well as the rest of the men and their stores. During the previous 5 months the front line squadrons had flown a total of almost 1500 hrs. There had been some 1350 sorties and over 1700 landings. These figures had never been passed in a similar period since *Melbourne* was first commissioned.

Jenny's Side Party

The minister of the Navy, Senator John Gorton, came aboard in the evening of the 14th June for the entry into Sydney, and the next day all ships and submarines linked up for the fleet entry into Sydney. We had friends and families of our Sydney crew at Garden Island to greet us. Several days after we had docked, a Bailey bridge was placed from the dockside onto the forward part of the flight deck to facilitate the de-storing and storing of *Melbourne*. While this was happening, interstate crew took 10 days mid-winter leave, including me. When I arrived back the ship was still undergoing maintenance.

Chapter 5

Gannets and Mishaps

S plicing the Mainbrace is a commemorative event set up to celebrate something special like the Queen's actual birthday, birth or marriage of royalty etc. On 10th July, 1961 I experienced one of these wonderful celebrations. It was the 50th Anniversary of the Royal Australian Navy. For those of us on duty though it was a 1 beer celebration, then back to work! After all we were back off to Jervis Bay, fully supplied on the 15th. The weather was rough this trip, so rough that the night flying exercises planned were held in Jervis Bay rather than out to sea. A Gannet aircraft was taxiing into a secure area (Fly One) when it skidded on the wet flight deck and its nose ended up in a gun sponson causing some damage to the aircraft and ship. The crew was lucky and escaped serious injury. Early the next day though when a demolition party was being landed at lighthouse jetty in Montagu Road,

Jervis Bay, Leading Seaman A. J. Moore was crushed between a workboat and the jetty and sadly this was one of those times where life did fall.

After a brief return to Sydney the ship headed to Hervey Bay to get the ship into shape for Admirals Inspection. In some ways it was a fairly boring stay here, no shore leave and about the only recreational pastime was fishing. Next day we took up anchor and headed out to sea for a brief exercise with the RAA, some of our ships and 2 of our submarines. After that it was off to the Steel Wharf in Brisbane. We had a wow of a time in Brisbane, having a couple of our crew as Brisbane-ites did help as they knew their way around and for nearly a week we found our way around. Then it was back out to sea again, exercise Tuckerbox and we made our way to Auckland NZ.

It was here in this fair city that a few of the flight deck crew were slipping ashore by whatever means were available to them – usually slipping down the bow line to get ashore. One member who got pretty tanked while ashore had quite a deal of trouble trying to make it back up the bow line so he went up the brow and was caught being ashore. The penalty for being caught ashore without leave or going up the bow line varied, but usually involved stoppage of leave, pay or a combination of all! It would have been a while before he did that again.

The Kiwis certainly made us all welcome. I remember there were cars lined up on the wharf for hours waiting to take the crew away for the weekend. There were plenty of parties around, but as I remember the beer left a lot to be desired as it was like coloured water to drink. There were also other dangers to drinking beer in NZ back then. When you walked into a bar the first thing that would catch your eye was someone at the bar with a demijohn filling it up with beer, even open top vessels. This was then used to fill the glasses, though sometimes people would take them home. The beer was brought to the pubs in tankers which would then fill up underground tanks. These tanks were made of wood and were not very well-made or looked after I would say, given the number of times I recall looking into the bottom of my glass to see small chips of wood!

After a brief stay in Wellington we headed into some pretty rough weather on our way home for a 5 day stay before going to Sydney — this time for a 3-month refit and a long wait for our leave, a whole 33 days at Christmas. Living on board ship during a refit is not the best. At times we had to go ashore just for the toilet facilities. Dirt and asbestos lay all around the decks as they pulled various areas apart. Thank goodness it didn't take that long for my leave to come around and I flew out of Sydney on the 29th November arriving home late that night. It was enjoyable and definitely better than living in the middle of a fit-out, but even on this leave I had some difficulty relating to everyone. Part of this stemmed from being in the 'Naval Family', I had grown apart from my family and friends who I left behind when I joined. What made it so was that in my case, indoctrination commenced the day I was sworn in, it's a different language, e.g., lunch is called 'scran', knife, fork and spoon are called 'fighting irons', the floor, deck, and ceiling are 'deckheads'. Things like this made it difficult to find things in common to talk about.

My posting was back to *HMAS Albatross* at Nowra where I was given the job of telephone switchboard operator. For the first couple of days it proved to be a rather daunting task. Mistakes I made plenty of but I was lucky, as there was always someone in the next room to help me out. The switchboard was in the main signal building, a highly classified security area. Here we would work (2 of us) 48hrs and 72hrs about with 2 others. This is where both Linton Ferguson and I got into big trouble and I would have to say that it was my fault. One weekend we were working on the afternoon watch from midday till 4 p.m. We had to log all outgoing calls which at times was a bit hard to do, so a lass from the Department of Works suggested that she teach us shorthand, which on that day she did. Unfortunately the duty regulating Petty Officer did his security check and behold, we were caught having a civilian in a secure area. Things didn't look too good for us. The end result was 14 days chooks (extra work out of working hours) and 21 days stoppage of leave and with the threat of having no mid-winter leave granted to us, though thankfully this did not occur.

Linton and I had a lot of fun that year. If we had been caught at some of it I know we would have been inside looking out. We would jump the fence, have a car stowed outside and go to Wollongong for a game of tenpin bowls. The lady Linton was courting at that stage would also come down and pick us up sometimes. It was surely my best time at *HMAS Albatross*. On the 25th of July I admitted myself to sick bay, having severe abdominal pain. The hospital doctor admitted me soon after and I would spend some 4 days in the hospital bed and as it turns out the only firm diagnosis was abdominal pain. (This problem would come to haunt me some years down the track).

Time went very quickly here even though we were all waiting to be posted out.

It was in the latter part of the year that the postings were out on the notice board and again I was posted to *HMAS Melbourne* to join by the 27th of December 1962. I had Christmas day at home as well as Boxing Day and travelled to Sydney the day after to board ship on the 27th.

Sydney was its usual boisterous city self during the New Year festivities. Kings Cross was full of people all out for a great night's fun. Then it was back to reality with the ship getting ready for sea trials and on the 4th January 1963, the *Melbourne* moved out to the buoy to bring on the stores like aviation fuel, ammo and general stores. We then headed back to sea on the 9th and it's interesting to note here that flight deck radiation trials were carried out and to date I can find no record of the results of those tests.

In 1964, the *HMAS Melbourne* and *HMAS Voyager* collided and the *Voyager* sank with many losing their lives. During 1963 there were 3 separate incidents that went very close to being collisions (listed below), but for the excellent seamanship of the *Melbourne's* bridge crew on each of those occasions. They were recorded in the Captains Report of Proceedings.

EXTRACT FROM REPORT OF PROCEEDINGS
FEB. 1963

Melbourne entered Port Philip heads at 0600hrs on Friday 15th. While passing through the dredged 'cut' at the eastern end of the south channel, the Lloyd Triestino vessel MV Australia passed between Melbourne and Quickmatch in formation and overhauled Melbourne at a speed very considerably in excess of the limit, passing dangerously close up Melbourne's side.

The Captain of *Melbourne* at this time was Capt. R Peek RAN. (Captain Peek went on to be Knighted Sir Richard Peek and was also one of the driving forces behind veterans involved in the Far East Strategic Reserve getting their veteran entitlements.)

EXTRACT FROM REPORT OF PROCEEDINGS
FEB. 1963

At the beginning of the month the ship was returning to Sydney, with Supply and ANZAC in company, on completion of a work up in the Jervis Bay area. While approaching Port Jackson, with ships formed in column, it was necessary to wheel 360 degrees to port to avoid the Matson Line vessel Monterey which, having stopped to embark a pilot, and therefore forfeiting her right of way, attempted to make the heads before warships in company.*

EXTRACT FROM REPORT OF PROCEEDINGS MARCH 1963
At 1200 hours on Thursday the 21st, Melbourne passed through the San Bernardino Strait and commenced the passage through the Philippine Islands unfortunately in very poor visibility. At 2225 hours the ship had to take violent avoiding action to evade an investigating patrol craft of the Philippine Navy later identified as PNS Capiz.

I've often wondered how many near misses were never recorded!

On the 5th of February we headed for Hobart with the promise of some 'natives' leave for all Tasmanian crew members. A few mates had been invited to my birthday which we had arranged to have at my sister's place. The hospitality of Hobart invaded my space on that weekend as most that were coming to the party were otherwise engaged, but Tubby Gilmore, Steve Brooks and a couple of other mates attended and we all had a great night. We left plenty of goods for my brother-in-law to quench his thirst on.

As always it's very hard to leave your home port but all the crew that I was close to were full of praise for the place. I got a fair bit of ribbing about the beer before we got to Hobart but not a whisper after we left. It ended up the best-tasting if not the strongest beer. Our next port of call after Hobart was close by, Melbourne, the big smoke. We stayed there till the 20th and then sailed again for Hobart, this time berthing at the Macquarie oil wharf. On Wednesday the 27th we had some flight deck drama. 'Cowboy' Keating who was one of the mobile crane drivers (Jumbo) tipped the crane on its side and in that same action he was thrown to the wharf some 40 feet below. Everyone expected broken bones so all were amazed that he walked away with only a broken finger! A very lucky man, our Cowboy. Before we left Hobart we went to see the poor Jumbocrane. It was a sight! There were 100 lashings tying it down so that it never moved anywhere again. It was during this visit to Hobart that the Queen was there as well but our paths didn't cross before we headed back to Sydney.

We again headed north on the 7^{th,} this time for Manus Island. During the approach to New Guinea, *Melbourne's* aircraft carried out tactical reconnaissance flights along the coasts of New Guinea, New Britain and off lying islands. It wasn't long before we would lose one of those aircraft while on a mission just off the northern end of Manus Island. Happily all the crew came out safe and sound. It was around this time that *Melbourne* had experienced some 20,000 aircraft landings, something to be very proud of.

We stayed in Manila Harbour for 4 days then up anchor and headed for Hong Kong. We arrived there early in April, staying for some 14 days. Everyone made their way ashore looking to buy goodies to take home. I bought a bit of gear, a bit more than my previous visit in 1961. One of the biggest problems that we faced on the flight deck was that during flying stations, because of a shortage of men, we were split up into 3 watches, two on and one off. This meant that during around-the-clock flying, out of the 24 hours, each watch would only get 8 hours off. It did take its toll on all of us as not only did we have to catch up on sleep, but also all our personal chores (washing, ironing etc.) had to be done.

HMAS Melbourne celebrating 20,000 landings.

I believe Martin Scott was the Flight Deck Officer during the '63 tour, however I am not sure who was the flight deck captain of that time. My memory says it may have been Eric Bush. We arrived in Singapore on the 20th and off-loaded 805 squadron and embarked RN squadron for a SEATO exercise, leaving Singapore on the 23rd. It seemed to be a year of incidents, if it wasn't the ship having near misses, we were having prangs with the aircraft. During the writing of my first book I had the good fortune to have correspondence with John van Gelder. John was a Gannet pilot in the Fleet

Air Arm and wrote an article that I had published in my first book and I thought it was pertinent that I should include it here as well.

CARRIER FLYING: THE GREATEST SPORT IN THE WORLD.

Some time ago, whilst having a drink in the bar of the local yacht club, I met a man whom I had never met before. In general conversation on learning that I had been a Fleet Air Arm pilot he said "…but that was a licence to kill yourself, wasn't it?" It was a ridiculous remark, however, I pondered later whether this may have been a general perception by people who should have known better.

By the time a pilot carries out his first deck landing he has undergone at least 2 years of fairly intensive academic and flying training and, in the process, seen about fifty per cent of his contemporaries fall by the wayside for various reasons. Before arriving at the aircraft carrier, the final intensive flying training schedule is devoted to ADDLs, or airfield dummy deck landings. This is the practice of being directed in the landing approach by a batsman. In my particular training, I recorded 212 ADDLS in Fairey Firefly aircraft at an airfield in Northern Ireland before my first deck landings on the great old aircraft carrier HMS Illustrious. By no stretch of the imagination could one suggest that we were under trained, nor that we were practising to "Kill ourselves".

Flying from straight deck carriers such as *HMA Illustrious* or *HMAS Sydney* and being "batted on" did have an element of risk and there was not really much margin for error. However, if you missed picking up one of the 9 arrester wires there were always the barriers to bring you to a stop. It was often said that there were 2 types of naval aviator- those that had been into the barrier and those that were going!

Strangely enough, one of the more difficult procedures I found operating from *HMAS Sydney* was taxiing the aircraft out of the Deck Park in order to get to the catapult. With the wings folded the aircraft always felt top heavy and inevitably the ship would be rolling whilst turning into wind. So at one moment one would be taxiing up hill and the next moment going downhill with some hapless aircraft handler frantically directing you to slow down before colliding with the Island.

Take off on the catapult was quite straightforward. Once the cockpit checks were done, the engines run up to take off power and the flight deck officers green flag went down you were going off the sharp end of the ship coming ready or not. The old hydraulic catapult gave quite an energetic kick initially and then slowed down. In fact on most occasions one could have the old Firefly airborne before reaching the end of the catapult.

Landing on was a different kettle of fish, you had to do it all by yourself with the aid of a batsman. The important thing was to set up the aircraft on the approach in the right attitude with wheels, hook and flaps down at the correct airspeed (92 knots for the Firefly) and follow signals from the batsman. The hardest part of this procedure was to ignore the movement of the flight deck if the ship was pitching to any extent. Once over the round down, the after end of the flight deck, and providing you had the 'roger' signal from the batsman followed by the 'cut' signal. All one had to do was to carry out a nice flared landing in among the arrestor wires and there you were — shaking, but safe at home! I always knew I was roughly in the right position for the 'cut' if the batsman's left hand disappeared between the fifth and sixth exhaust stubs on the port side.

By the late 1950s everything changed. With the acquisition of *HMAS Melbourne* we had an aircraft carrier with an angled flight deck, a mirror landing system, a steam catapult and new aircraft. One thing that did not change was the sporting element associated with the whole operation since now we had the opportunity to demonstrate how clever we were by flying throughout the night as well as by day. Whoever said, "The more light, less fright" was absolutely spot-on.

For carrier operations the de Havilland Sea Venom and the Fairey Gannets had one very great advantage over their predecessors, the forward was excellent. Unfortunately, both aircraft had certain disadvantages and in both cases they were somewhat under powered, particularly for hot tropical operations.

The Gannet was generally regarded as a 'gentleman's' aircraft to fly. As an anti-submarine aircraft it was, without doubt, very effective, as a deck landing aircraft, with its excellent forward vision and good engine response it made life relatively easy. The Gannet was a twin turbo prop aircraft fitted with the Armstrong Siddeley Double Mamba engine. This engine was beautifully made with the care of a Swiss watchmaker. When working it worked well, however, there were always the niggling doubts in the pilots' minds that it may not keep on working. Single engine landings on the carrier were not something that pilots looked forward to, particularly in the tropics.

To my mind the Sea Venom was a delight to fly and had no particular vices. The centrifugal flow turbo jet engine was very robust, reliable and almost unbreakable. A deck landing with the Venom was not difficult, primarily due to the excellent forward vision. However, the key to success in this procedure was to start the final approach in the right position with the aircraft in the correct altitude and the right air speed (about 112 knots). Then all one had to do was fly the mirror to finish up in the arrestor wires. Strangely enough, I found it easier to land the Venom than the Gannet. The reason being that because of the faster approach speed, you had less time to make mistakes! Unfortunately, I did not get around to deck landing the Venom at night.

Flying from the *Melbourne* in the tropics on a moonlight night, at 1000 feet above sea, in tropical haze, with no visible horizon, flying on instruments was not what I would call a recipe for a fun evening. But, then, I suppose someone had to do it.

Some people may regard all the above to be a little glamorous, and in some ways it may have been. However, it was all made possible by the hard work and dedication of many people operating within the ship. I have always had the greatest respect and admiration for the personnel who worked on the flight deck during flying operations. Who can forget the stokers who lay under the aircraft on the catapult attaching the strop to the aircraft, and the catapult shuttle with propellers whirling and jet exhaust blast only feet away and aircraft handlers directing aircraft on the flight deck by day and night and standing only feet away from menacing propellers. The aircrews placed their trust in all the people and were never let down. In respect of trust, in all the time I had flying in the RAN not once did I ever doubt that our aircraft were maintained to the absolute highest standards that could be found anywhere in the world.

As a footnote, the Oxford dictionary defines 'Sport' as '...a game or competitive activity...' and yes it was 'the greatest sport in the world' although it may have been a long time ago the memories are still vivid.'

John van Gelder
Commander RAN Rtd.
Sydney Feb.2000

It is with some sadness we lost John van Gelder a couple of years ago, a great loss.

Here are just 2 of the incidents involving Gannet aircraft in 1963.

EXTRACT FROM REPORT OF PROCEEDINGS FOR THE MONTH OF APRIL 1963

At 1620hours the port engine of Gannet 816 failed just after the aircraft had been launched. The aircraft had insufficient height to gain speed and ditched ahead of the ship. The crew, Lieutenant (SL) N Dennett (P), Lieutenant (SL) P Moy (O), and Lieutenant (SL) H Beardsall (O) were unhurt, one being picked up rescue helicopter and the other 2 by Melbourne's sea boat.

EXTRACT FROM REPORT OF PROCEEDINGS FOR THE MONTH OF MAY.

On the afternoon of Friday the 3rd, during a sortie in this exercise, a Gannet aircraft piloted by Lieutenant (SL) WP James reported engine failure at a distance of 90 miles from the ship and Melbourne and Yarra proceeded immediately to its assistance. On one engine, with reduced power and very low oil pressure, the pilot succeeded in returning his aircraft to the ship and carried out a landing with only partial power on the one engine available. The pilot's skill and tenacity in bringing the aircraft safely back on board enabled the defect in the gear train to be analysed and a modification was developed. While this was in hand it was necessary to ground all Gannet aircraft and they were unable to play any further part in the exercise.

Chapter 6

The Closeness of War.

EXTRACT FROM SHIP'S LOG MONDAY 20TH MAY 1963.
0200HOURS ASSUMED 3RD DEGREE OF READINESS
0215HOURS ASSUMED ABCD STATE 2 CONDITION 1
1000 HOURS ACTION GUN CREWS CLOSE UP.
1015 HOURS REVERT TO ABCD STATE 3 CONDITION X
1020 HOURS ACTION GUN CREWS FALL OUT.GUNS UNLOADED.
EXTRACT FROM REPORT OF PROCEEDINGS FOR THE MONTH OF MAY 1963.
PASSAGE EXERCISES WERE AGAIN KEPT TO A MINIMUM SO THAT TRAINING FOR ADVANCEMENT MIGHT BE PROGRESSED. ON PASSAGE THROUGH THE SUNDRE STRAIT EARLY ON THE MORNING OF THE 20TH THE SHIP ASSUMED THE 3RD DEGREE

OF A.A. READINESS AND WARTIME CRUISING CONDITIONS.

Flying was around the clock and out of every 24 hours we had 8 hours off watch to do all our own personal chores as well as getting as much sleep as possible.

It came very apparent prior to starting this book when I perused the documentation on *HMAS Melbourne* for the year of 1961 that the Captain never gave anything away to us, the crew, on security matters. I have since discovered that *HMAS Melbourne*, like the other ships carrying the Australian flag, did their own bit of intelligence gathering. It carried the name The Third Wireless, yet this fact never saw the light of day until a few years ago. This also I feel showed that *Melbourne* like the other ships was 'operational' during the times in South East Asia. The ship along with those that took part in the SEATO exercise arrived in Manila Bay on the 8th before touring around the region making brief stopovers.

From the time I wrote the detail above I have been investigating and searching for details in regard to that day, and it has surprised me what has come to fruition. From my submissions to the Commonwealth Government I found both ignorance and a lack of knowledge of the RAN's service during the 50s and the 60s. There also is the perception that we don't want to offend the Indonesian Government, but what some of the government has to learn is that peace always comes at a cost, and when payment is due it should be forthcoming.

Everything was full-on and fair dinkum. I have often wondered why the push was on to go through the Sunda Strait at that point of time when the order was to not intimidate the Indonesians. There was a 12-mile territorial zone from Land's End out to sea set by the Indonesians. This was not recognised by the opposing forces during the Indonesian Confrontation. The *HMAS Yarra* was our backup/support vessel. She was a quarter of our size but could turn on a sixpence which made her more than capable of looking after us. However she had been sent away to Christmas Island. My research since has shown that she was sent there because an Indonesian submarine was in the area trying to stop us getting through the Straits, but at the time none of this information was made available to us. It left us in a vulnerable position — as we saw it — with no backup if we needed it.

We arrived back in Fremantle on the 25th of May, dropping the West Australians off for their mid-winter leave, then on again we headed for Melbourne. It was time for mid-winter leave for some. The next day the rest of us made our way for Sydney after taking on wartime stores. The ship immediately went into a long self-maintenance period. It was a bit of an obstacle course to find your way around the ship, bits of pipe and lagging, a fair bit of a mess at the best of times. The routine was pretty mundane with a quick trip to Hervey Bay for Admiral's Inspection then back to Sydney for a short stay, then down Jervis Bay for a work up. On one of my afternoon trips ashore in Sydney I visited a pub in the Darlinghurst area and after a while there, I moved out of the place only to be met by 2 policemen. They said I was drunk and with one on either side of me, escorted me to the lockup. Four hours in the 'can' for 'drunk and disorderly' and a 10 shillings fine. I still have a bit of a laugh about it. Then it was back to routine, exercises and refits. The ship was even fumigated one weekend. Everyone had to go ashore that time — they used arsenic 'bombs'!

My new posting for 1964 was to *HMAS Harman* near Canberra. I had been looking for something new and here it was. Before settling in though, we had Christmas leave. A few of us had booked to travel on the Southern Aurora for our Christmas leave. We only had to pay the difference between first and second class and the extra was well worth it. It was on this leave that Trevor and his soon-to-be-wife were to be married at Strahan on the West Coast. I was asked to be their groomsman and was very pleased to oblige. It meant an 8-hour bus trip from Hobart to Queenstown, then another hour or more to Strahan but well worth it. The wedding went off well and everyone had a good time. I stayed in Queenstown for about a week looking around, with a bit of romance in the interim then on to Devonport for another week. It was probably the best leave time I'd had and it went very quickly. It seemed that I was back on the plane and heading back across the Strait before I knew it. Sadly, recently I received a phone call from Joy, Trevor's wife, who gave me the bad news that Trevor had cancer and it was terminal. We have been close for more than fifty years. I've lost many mates over the years and the

Navy family has always been strong and close, but it's still hard when one leaves.

I arrived in Canberra on the 5th of January 1964 and never having been there before I was a little lost, to say the least. *HMAS Harman* was only a small shore establishment compared to say *Albatross*. One soon got into the swing of the routine though. The town of Queanbeyan was just across the border in New South Wales and we would cross the border many times in the year to come.

What really stood out here was the Junior Ranks Club. It had a very social outlook in all respects. There were over a hundred members. A lot of the crew here worked either in Navy Office or one of the communication establishments close by. Here there was a very real sense of social harmony, everyone went out of his or her way to make one feel at home.

The month of February would have an enormous impact on the whole country, even more on the naval establishment with the collision of *HMAS Melbourne* and *HMAS Voyager* off Jervis Bay. We were all in a state of shock for several days, especially those of us who had so recently served on either ship. There were recriminations from many directions but we who served continued on with what we knew best and that was always giving our best at all times.

It would be 40-plus years before it would again be a part of my life. In September 2006 I received correspondence from "Hollows" lawyers seeking my input at the Supreme Court in Launceston where the trial of a bloke I had joined up with was set to appear seeking compensation in regards to his role in the collision of *HMAS Melbourne* and *HMAS Voyager*. I knew Geoffrey very well and expressed that view at the trial. He was granted compensation, but one has to wonder why it took so long and why so difficult as now there are other problems arising from the complexities of that settlement. He was very much a changed man from the one I knew, he drank to excess and smoked. It wasn't hard to see the effect the incident had had on his life, and he continues to have health problems that affect his lifestyle.

It was also that same year by general consensus we agreed to play rugby league, a social inter-ship competition. This was always classed as a professional sport and from the offset there were those that did not agree at all with the decision to play it. Ken Donnelly led the push to play the game and he could have also led the push to have a coach from the Queanbeyan Leagues Club comes out and coach us. I have to say that I didn't have a clue about this type of football or for that matter any game of football, but it was fun. It didn't stop me taking an early mid-winter leave to go home to help my brother and his fiancée celebrate their engagement though. While there I met a young woman that took my eye and a close relationship developed. My most dramatic entry and exit in a game was against a local Batemans Bay side. Very early in the game the other side were playing very rough and our coach had the ref. pull the game up and in so many words said, 'If these fellows want to fight we will fight or if they want play footy we will, which is it?' They agreed to play footy! Just into the game again, I was kicked in the head. It was no one's fault, just the run of play but I was out for the rest of the game. The story does not end there. After the game we all went down to the beach and had a few beers and it was while I was in the water I was bitten by something in the water. It didn't take long for the poison to work on me as I fell into a heap on the ground. I was taken to the Batemans Bay Hospital and here my carers were instructed to place me on a trolley which immediately collapsed. Somehow the trolley and the lead to the steriliser had become entangled. Lucky for me it had not been turned on! It was still full of water, cold water, and it ended up all over me. I had the hospital staff worried for a short time, but they discharged me. I was taken back to *HMAS Harman* and attempted to carry on with my normal duties but it wasn't for long. A dizzy spell soon had me knocking on the hospital door and I was admitted with concussion. I would spend a week in the base hospital under the great care of the staff.

During the year we invited various crews of the ships that came to Sydney to come down for the weekend. They would be invited to supply a footy team and we would make sure that they had a great weekend. I might say here we went unbeaten throughout that year. There was support in setting up the football competition properly, even calling it the Molonglo Shield, after a local river if I remember correctly.

My romance continued at a pleasant pace, the lady in my life came to visit for 2 weeks, which was very good for me and it wasn't long before the posting schedule was out on the notice board. My next posting was back to *HMAS Melbourne* on the 7th of Dec. My 14 days at home went too quickly for everyone concerned, but I have to say I was a little puzzled with the quietness of my lady friend. I was placed at arm's length on several occasions.

I arrived back in Sydney on the 7th of December. It seemed kind of strange this time around, not being home for at least part of the festive season, but there was always plenty of activity in and around the big smoke. It was at about this time of the year we were all given our areas of duty during flying operations. Mine was a two-part role. One was on take-off where I would assist the Flight Deck Officer adjacent to the catapult and during the landing on of aircraft I would be on the mirror landing platform assisting the Mirror Landing Officer checking the aircraft during their final approach that everything appeared to be correct for landing on. It looked like a big year was on the way as *Melbourne* slipped away from the wharf on the 4th of Jan.1965 to the buoy to load ammunition and stores. Then we were off to Jervis Bay area for a work up and to continue cleaning the ship.

The ship continued its work-ups and exercises between Sydney and Jervis Bay till the end of January. The changeover in the crew was well over 80%.

Early on in the trip to Hobart we lost our first aircraft for the year. It had a total power loss after take-off and the crew ditched the aircraft about 500 yards from the ship. Luckily they were rescued wet and unhurt in quick time by the SAR helicopter. The ship's crew had a great stay in Hobart as always. Everyone was made very welcome. Even my lady friend was friendlier. We left Hobart on the 11th and made for Sydney and it was at this time that the rumour mill was full on. It appeared that the civilian population knew more than we did, where we were going and when. Vietnam was the cry. On the 23rd we moved back out to the buoy to bring on freight ammunition for Singapore.

Obviously though not all the natives of Hobart were friendly. A rifle bullet had passed through the Interrogator Aerial mounted on the masthead. The actual time of the event was unknown, but, from the downward angle of the hole and the penetration, it may well have occurred in Hobart where the ship was berthed below a hill.

Chapter 7

Problems Continue.

EXTRACT FROM REPORT OF PROCEEDINGS MARCH 1965

During transit of the Celebes Sea (0800K Friday 5th March to 8th March) defence stations were assumed in accordance with CTG 327.2 Opord 1/65. No incidence occurred.

The ship chopped to the operational control of COMFEF at 0001Z Saturday 6th March.

This is the point where the British took command of the fleet. On Sunday the 7th there was another close call with a Gannet aircraft whilst airborne. There was a fire in the port engine and pilot 'Tos' Dadswell somehow brought it in for a successful single engine landing. While we were in Singapore in late April 1965, it was a very busy time. A short time after securing to C Buoy, Dockyard Reach Singapore, and the dive team received a number of air bottles from HMS Terror (Singapore Naval Base) after being refilled in case they may be required during their stay in Singapore. Needless to say, later that night they were ordered to do a bottom search for mines, and this was no exercise.

Bottom lines were rigged. These go from one side of the ship, underneath, and are tied in predetermined places. Divers operate in pairs using a lightweight line which they attach to the bottom line, then it is pulled tight and attached to the other bottom line. They then use these lines to help with their search and help each other should it be needed. There is another diver working the lines above the surface. At this time the Captain ordered sentries to be posted around the ship as all divers wore overalls and were only armed with a knife.

At 0040 hrs on the 30th April there were bubbles reported in the starboard section which resulted in the divers being called out with boat crews. Harry Harkness was one of those divers. As a result of checking the hull for mines and searching for intruding divers, Harry (and I'm sure others would have had similar experiences) nearly lost his life. His airline became twisted around the swim line. It was pitch black, but luckily his partner used the swim line to find him. He cut the airline to free Harry and supported him up to the surface.

I must mention that Harry states in his book "Onus Of Proof" that the Ship's Company had little regard for what the divers were doing, I have to repudiate that by saying if the Ship's Company had known what the divers were doing and why, the divers would have had all the support that would be needed. Here in situations like this the blame must stay with the top brass. Many ex-naval men when seeking compensation have set precedents through the various levels of the court system.

Melbourne slipped from the buoy at 0800hrs on the 15th and proceeded for FOTEX '65' in the Malacca Strait area. All the ships anchored off Langkawi from the 19th to the 22nd for briefings, drills and some recreational leave ashore. We had had a pretty hard week, so an afternoon ashore was something to look forward to. We were allowed to take our beer ration (one can) ashore with us under supervision, and it was to be distributed when we got ashore. Sadly, that did not happen, our beer was given to the Master at Arms (Naval Policeman). Luckily the Poms had NAFFI ashore with beer so we ended up OK! On returning to the ship a little the worst for wear, we vented our feelings to those concerned.

During the second phase of the Fotac we lost another aircraft with a tragic ending.

At 0431 Wednesday 24 March during participation in Fotac Two Gannet 811 crashed over the side after landing on in position 5Degrees 58'N 99Degrees 10.5E resulting in the presumed death of the pilot Acting Sub/ Lieutenant (SL) J.M. Hutchinson (P) RAN. Search was abandoned after 4 ½hrs. Full details have been reported separately and the accident has been investigated by the board of inquiry convened Melbourne on Monday 28 and Tuesday 29. (Report of Proceedings)

I recall that just prior to the crash there was a voice from Flyco calling a MAY DAY! MAY DAY! It turned out later that it was a British helicopter.

Until recently I always thought that there was only the pilot in that aircraft and that was John Hutchison in the Gannet aircraft that crashed over the side of *HMAS Melbourne*. Recently others have verified that my perception had been wrong. There were 2 other crew members in the aircraft when it landed. As it landed there was a problem with the hook when catching the wire. It broke. The 2 co-pilots escaped onto the deck but not John Hutchinson. He was the only one not able to leave it before it went over the side. They later found only his helmet.

During the early part of April, the ship arrived in Hong Kong for a short self-maintenance period. As always, when a ship first arrives in port everyone is waiting on the mail arrival, the end of the sorting, and the distribution. To my surprise I received a registered parcel. I'm sure Marie after 40 odd years would realise that in retrospect she was right in breaking off the engagement. Reflecting on the past of many of those that served, there had been so many relationships broken because of the long separation. The contents at the time though shocked me for some considerable time.

It was a 'Dear John', a brief note to say our engagement was off and the engagement ring was in the parcel as well. I was angry and distressed. I had sensed something was wrong when I had been home last but never expected this. She had my car and my bankbook also! Luckily she couldn't draw anything from it. This left me with a great distrust of the opposite sex, and I stayed away from any new relationship for a long time. While it upset me at the time I did get over it and my hope is that she went on to a great relationship with the bloke she left me for and is as happy as I am. Life does present these sort of difficulties to us whenever we least expect them.

During the early part of our stay in Hong Kong, I was inducted into the Royal Order of Antediluvian Buffaloes, Grand Australasian Banner with quite a few of the blokes I knocked around with. It's a bit of a mouthful but most of the blokes that I had knocked around with at this time were there for the big occasion. It was all a bit of fun and kept us occupied but I don't have much to do with them now.

We left Hong Kong on the 21st and headed south to Singapore. The intelligence network was at work too with a report of 2 Russian freighters in the neighbourhood and one would not have to think very far forward to guess at their heading — North Vietnam. An air search was carried out for the 2 vessels in question but as it turned out they were well out of our search area.

We arrived in Singapore on the 27th and after several days we again moved, this time with the compass lined up for Manila. We were attached to a task force doing an exercise and at the same time heading for Bangkok arriving there on the 22nd of May. I was on duty the first night in and was made part of the duty shore patrol. The ships were anchored out for our stay here and for any of our crew to get into Bangkok they had to get a bus and these were allocated to the various ships.

We received word that an American serviceman was on one of the Australian buses and making a fair bit of noise. The American shore patrol told us they would handle him on the bus arriving back and handle him they did. Rather roughly to say the least. It was pouring with rain at the time and he was left in the gutter and they came back for him later. The ship sailed again on the 25th for what we originally thought was to be a couple of ports in Japan. The rumour mill was fairly rife ever since we left Sydney and even then it was all around that we were going to Vietnam.

It was in May 1965, prior to the departure of *HMAS Sydney* to Vietnam with the first Australian Army Battalion, that John P. van Gelder was invited to write the Directive (rules of engagement) for the HMA Ships and RAAF Maritime patrol aircraft involved in the operation. He personally wrote the Directive which was signed by the Chief of Naval Staff and Chief of Air Staff, who passed it to the Department of Defence who in turn presented it to Federal Cabinet on Friday afternoon 24th May 1965 (Senator Shane Paltridge was Minister for Defence). It was approved unaltered by Cabinet and released as Top Secret (exclusive) signal on Friday night. *HMAS Sydney* sailed for Vietnam on the 25th May. The document that I have recently received from Dr. John Carroll described it as 'Standing Orders for *HMAS Sydney* and escorts for Vietnam voyages'. I have to admit after reading it, the main emphasis is with regard to the *Sydney* and her close-in escorts in and around Vung Tau. However, we prepared for war, went as far as South Vietnam and were in Vietnam waters several times with *HMAS Sydney* but we were then sent on other exercises.

It was the 4th of June that we first joined *HMAS Sydney* together with *HMAS Duchess* and *Parramatta*. Defence stations were assumed at 0001hrs that morning. From here it would be a four-day journey to South Vietnam. One Wessex helicopter operated as a screen role for the next 3 days and this was to increase once the ship cleared the Balabac Strait. There was a Gannet fixed wing aircraft on patrol during daylight hours. Sea Venom aircraft were also flown on dawn and dusk probe missions when the wind conditions were favourable.

Whilst *HMAS Melbourne* continued the role of escorting *Sydney, Melbourne* continued to zigzag when not operating aircraft. This is one of the tactics used in anti-submarine warfare. There has been very little revealed as to the role and the results of it as well. One can only assume that time will allow that to happen. There has always been that veil of secrecy around whatever and where-ever the ship moved to and from. My main reason for putting the previous information in is that there has been, to this day, very little if no recognition of the role taken by the ship and its crew and the only difference between them is in this one we never reached the war zone. At the end of the day all the same planning and all that goes with it is there and yet still no recognition, even though we were in Vietnamese waters during war time. I leave it up to the reader to reach a conclusion.

The ship arrived back in Sydney on the 22nd of June and on arrival the bulk of the crew went on 10 days mid-winter leave.

This was a very hard period for me, after arriving in Hobart I got the bus service to New Norfolk to pick up my car and what other chattels Marie may have chosen to give back to me. As it turns out, all I got was my car and a suitcase with my old steam and dry iron inside. We did not part on very good terms. Those 10 days went very quickly for me. I went out, got drunk and stayed that way until I had to return to work.

Several weeks after my return from leave, I got a posting for a class 1 driver's course. This course was fairly intense, 6 weeks long with learning to drive anything from a staff car to a 42-seat bus, as well as understanding the mechanics of them all. There was also a 50-question exam on rules of the road. Here one was only allowed to get 2 questions wrong, any more and you failed the whole course, which at the end of the day is how it should be.

The unavailability of Bretts Wharf in Brisbane prevented *HMAS Melbourne* remaining in Brisbane until Tuesday 14th September when the ship was scheduled to sail in company with *HMAS Sydney* prior to proceeding to South Vietnam. ANZAC joined us on the 14th then all set sail for the Grafton Passage. Once clear of the Grafton Passage at noon on Thursday the 16th, the ships acted in accordance with CTF 327 Op Order 12/65, promulgated by FOCAF Message 060245z September. Two Wessex in the screening role were kept continuously on task from 1300 Thursday 16th until 1300 Friday 17th September. Gannets were employed in ASW and surface search at dusk and dawn and in a search of the China Strait area.

Time seemed to go very quickly and in no time the ship was back in Sydney and into refit. The Christmas break came early for a good many of us as we headed home on the 6th of December. The home that I arrived at was very different to the one that I had left some 6 months ago. Dad picked me up from the bus and one of the first things he said to me was, 'I'm glad you're home, maybe you can help me, your mother has not spoken to me for a month and I don't really know why.' Sadly I was no help as she stayed in much the same mood during my entire time home. It finally became apparent to me that the family unit as I understood it was not as steady as I'd thought and my youngest brother was having problems too. He had not attended school at all during his teen years. He wanted to go to work and so he did. My guess is that the problems that he now faced were in part because of that decision to leave school so early, (against our parents' wishes). He was a bit of a rebel and landed himself in trouble quite a few times. My sister Valerie had also left home some time before this because of a dispute with the family but there was now another change. She and her husband, Vince, had split, the reason for which may never be known to us. Mother did come around, but it was a slow process for all concerned and we never knew what caused the original problem. It was one of a very few times that I would spend Christmas Day and New Year at home and it was not the happiest.

Early January, 1966 saw me re-join *HMAS Melbourne* with the refit not yet finished. This was mainly due to union strictures and a lack of experienced Dockyard Laggers. The work also had to be done when machinery was closed up and other trades were not working in the vicinity. Finally, at the end of January, the ship finally went out to sea for a final shake down. The flight deck crew had a busy day on the 24th of February with a May Day call from a Wessex in the morning landing safely and a short time later a Gannet declared a 'Pan' (emergency landing for a minor malfunction) and also landed safely. While night flying, a Gannet crashed over the port side. Happily the crew got out unhurt but we could not save the aircraft. After some continued workup as well as in and out of *Sydney*, it was on the 24th of March that the ship sailed for northern ports but again there was an adverse health report underway.

Chapter 8

Health and Morale

The health of the Ship's Company is generally good. However during the month too many people continued to suffer with sore throats and upper respiratory throat infections. It is considered that dirty ventilation may be the cause.

On Monday 28th March a major compound fracture was successfully managed in the sick bay while on Tuesday a case of appendicitis was transferred to HMAS Yarra and successfully operated upon. Both patients are recovering satisfactorily; the former being transferred to Rabaul hospital by helicopter on arrival there.

On the way to meeting up with *HMAS Sydney* we called into Singapore for a short stay, leaving there on the 18th and back in again on the 21st. Moving out again on ANZAC Day the 25th.

At 1501H Thursday 28 April during flying operations in the Sulu Sea, Sea Venom WZ 900 crashed over the side after landing on in position 08 degrees 12'.ON 118 degrees 16'.8E, resulting in the presumed death of the observer, Lieutenant (X) (o) E. G. Kennell RAN. A search of the area by HMAS Yarra was abandoned after 3 ½ hr.

Full details have been reported separately and the Board of inquiry convened in HMAS Melbourne on Friday 29th April has investigated the accident.

This accident was to have a great bearing on my life many years later, and it would cause me to have flashbacks continuously for a long time. During the 1966 tour, my role in flying operations was in the Aircraft Control Room assisting the Aircraft Control Room Officer, Lt. John Elliott, but on this day I was called in to fill in on the Mirror Control Area platform during the landing on of Sea Venom 900 WZ. It was a very dramatic few seconds. I had previously given the OK to the Mirror Control Officer that it was all clear for the aircraft to land on. He was yelling into the RT in his headset and I was doing much the same but the aircraft noise was drowning us both out.

For such a long time the memory of that event above most other things in my life, remained up front in my memory and of course at times I found it very difficult to deal with. I recall rushing up the deck to where the aircraft went over the angle deck and saw the few remains of the aircraft on the water with Ted Kennell appearing to be still attached to his ejection seat – and it was beginning to sink. I do recall one member of the flight deck crew asking for permission to jump in and save him. The Flight Deck Officer replied "Permission denied". On reflection it was the right reply, we would have lost 2 that day otherwise.

There may be others who will give a different view of those events and that is their right. I suppose, my only question is that considering my role at that time, I was never asked any questions by the board of inquiry. Here again I have to ask, why not?

Flying operations were suspended during the board of inquiry and the ship continued on an uneventful passage across the Sulu Sea and through the Basilan Straits towards the rendezvous.

Defence stations were assumed from 0800h Saturday 30th April and the rendezvous with HMAS Sydney and HMAS Vampire were made at 1345H 30th April.

A helo lift of main and stores took place from HMAS Sydney while she was refuelling from HMAS Supply. On completion of the replenishment, HMAS Supply detached and the remainder of the force proceeded towards Vietnam at speed in advance of 171/2 Knots

The month of April ended with HMAS Melbourne in the Eastern Celebes Sea proceeding in accordance with the route laid down in FOCAF real link Op. Order 5/66, promulgated by signal DTG 060028z April. The Ship's

Company were at condition One and *Gannet* aircraft carried out a surface search at dawn and dusk.

In between the entire ongoing rumour mill, the health of the Ship's Company was always in question as the Senior Medical Officer reported.

> 'The health of the Ship's Company is in general good, but there has been some deleterious effect from the prolonged spell of hot humid conditions without air conditioners. Dehydration and alteration of body functions manifest this.
> On the 26th May an officer who had been sick since 20th May was clinically diagnosed as suffering from typhoid fever. Confirmation of this could not be made with the facilities available on board. He was landed at Subic Bay and subsequent intensive laboratory investigation carried out by the USN medical department indicates that he has a Viral Infective Mononucleosis, although the possibility of it being typhoid is not entirely excluded.
> In belief that the ship might be quarantined on arrival in Sydney with a communicable disease, a request for assistance to identify a typhoid carrier was made to the Medical Director General. Surgeon Commander SJ Lloyd RAN was flown to Manila and joined the ship on the 31st.'
> The health of the Ship's Company is adversely affected by the bad living, working and sleeping conditions in the ship in tropical service. Several instances of mild to severe heat exhaustion have occurred in machinery space watch-keepers.

> *The daily attendance of sailors with upper respiratory tract infections, headaches and diarrhoea due to poor habitability has been greater than usual.*

[There were much deeper medical reports made by the Fleet Medical Officer which warrants reading as it gives more and better information. I have added these at the end for those interested in reading more.]

My most vivid memory of the escort trips to Vietnam was one day just as it was breaking dawn. *HMAS Melbourne* was fairly close in shore and 2 American jet aircraft were flying on shore dropping napalm bombs; it was a very dramatic sight.

It wasn't long before we again picked up *HMAS Sydney*. This time she had *HMAS Vendetta* with her as the other escort into South Vietnam. We did a lot of escort duty around Vietnam in '65 and '66.

The routine set out by FOCAF for the escort of *HMAS Sydney* was similar as the previous trips with dawn to dusk searches by fixed wing aircraft, with Wessex Helicopters at 'Condition One'. The Ship's Company was in defence watches. This work did seem to be and was an everyday routine but with one big difference, that was, there was a war going on out there, and not too far away. With that in mind we had to be aware of all contingencies that could prevail. With this job done it was time for us to make a heading for home, firstly Fremantle in the west.

On leaving the west we headed across the Great Australian

Bight and what a trip that turned out to be — very rough for a couple of days. I was a bit reluctant to go on holidays this time around not knowing what was on or off the boil at home. What I did find was that there would always be some changes that would affect a lot of people for the rest of their lives. This is where my mate Trevor took a tumble in the forward lift well and it shook him up a little. I took 10 days leave on the 9th of July and arrived back in Sydney on the 20th.

During the remainder of the year *Melbourne* was either having maintenance done or in and out of Sydney on exercise. It was fairly late in the year when I again was posted to *HMAS Harman* in the ACT. I left *HMAS Melbourne* for the last time on the 10th of December for 30 days leave. It was with some sadness that I left 'The Melbourne' as the Fleet Air Arm had been a big part of my life and to leave it, was like leaving part of my family behind. It turned out to be a pretty lonely period for me. It seemed that it was only a few days and I was back in an aircraft and winging my way back to Canberra. My job this time was driving — any vehicle that was in the pool.

HMAS Harman was probably the best shore base that I had served in. Unlike any of the others, this one did not have a wet mess but a club. I had only been there a couple of weeks and was asked to take on the position of Secretary of the Club. I did it with gusto. Needless to say I was a frequent visitor to the club rooms. We had many functions; it was a club with great atmosphere, the envy of many people, not discounting the officers (they were only allowed by invitation).

Towards the end of May, I received a letter from my eldest

sister asking me why I hadn't been home to see my mother as she had spent some time in hospital with a heart problem. I had no prior knowledge of my mother's problem otherwise I would have been in contact with them earlier. I have to say, I did not behave myself very well because of the news. I drank too much and needless to say got into trouble resulting in the stoppage of club privileges for the duration of my time at *Harman*. After some discussion with the Welfare Officer at that time, I received an emergency posting to the Naval Shore base in Hobart as Captain's driver.

Chapter 9

Returning Home

I landed back in Hobart for my leave on the 26th of June with little fanfare. I joined *HMAS Huon* on the 9th of July meeting the 11 crew as well as the Captain, Commander Ian Hutchinson and his wonderful wife, both made me very welcome. In conversation he told me that he had flown in squadrons with Douglas Bader during the Second World War.

The captain put it to me many times that I should sign on for another 3 years but my 9 years were up and I had had enough. I no longer found the same satisfaction working for the Navy. I just wanted to work out my time, then leave. I continually refused the offer. My job was to take the skipper to his office in the morning and pick him up at night, and probably do safe-hand mail runs to the airport. Also I would do the shopping for the kitchen and any other job that came up as well as being on call. It all kept me pretty busy most of the time. Another part of my role was to assist the captain and place wood in his home and set their fires for him and his wife. Most times I would be asked by Mrs. Hutchinson to stay for a cup of tea and a chat. One great lady, she made me very welcome.

The Executive Officer did not appreciate it at all; we never hit it off. This also was part of my reason for not signing on for another 3 years. I do recall he always addressed me by my surname 'Browning' and this did irk me. He did say to me one day, 'Browning, why don't you call me Sir?' Well, my answer was obvious, 'I too have a title, use it.' Time soon passed for me and it did not take long before it was time for me to get my house in order, re my discharge medical etc. On reflection, the medical was of a pretty sparse nature, quick and not very deep. I was a little surprised considering my service medical background, but after talking to some of the other blokes I learnt that much the same happened to them.

Leaving the Naval Family was a hard thing for me to do, even today I still have some regrets about it all. I didn't put much effort into lining a job up before it was time for me to leave either; I'm not sure why.

I had 14 days leave left, so that meant that I could finish my time a little early. I said my few goodbyes and left on the 9th February, 1968 and headed home.

I found home a very lonely place, even though there were always plenty of people around. The biggest problem that I had was the language barrier, some people may find that statement funny to say the least, but servicemen and women do have a very different language version of our language. I had worn a uniform for 9 years and had in essence been indoctrinated with the Naval jargon and it's something that sticks to you for the rest of your life.

I found it very hard to settle into the way of civilian life; it had no discipline, at least none that I had been used to.

Boredom was my worst enemy. I had been so used to a routine every day, now I didn't have the resources to change it all. With being so bored I very soon found an outlet to fill that void and that was a frequent visit to one of the local pubs and take some alcohol home till my next visit to the pub.

I believe it was my mother who eventually said to me, 'Get off your backside and go out and get a job'. This was some 6 months after I had been discharged.

The fallout from Vietnam was starting to take off with protests and the media write-ups. It was not a time for anyone to say that they had any involvement in the Vietnam War and that's really what it was: a war. Some of our men were coming home in body bags, and no, it's not the nicest way of putting it either. Body bags are body bags and they carried the remains of our men home from South East Asia and other parts of the world.

As it would turn out, the Vietnam War would claim the lives of several blokes that I had served with at some time or another. I did not say anything to anyone about my involvement except that it was in the role of escorting the *Sydney* in and out of Vietnamese waters. Here history will tell the story that quite a lot of Vietnam veterans never let it be known what their background was and some who tried to join the local branch of the RSL were knocked back. Sadly this was also said to some Second World War veterans when they returned.

In March 1968, the Defence Department sent me a letter asking me would I join the newly formed Emergency Naval Reserve and with the money they were offering I jumped at it. This entailed giving 13 days a year for training anywhere around the country. I did around 7 different periods of service in the Emergency Reserve. One at *HMAS Lonsdale* at Port Melbourne was memorable. The Melbourne Cup was on and I joined a group of good people that I had teamed up with over the preceding years and went to Flemington Racecourse for the day. What a day it was!

We had all met in the 'paddock' which as I recall was just near the winning post. I backed the winner Van Der Hum; mind you we all got a very wet backside, as it rained cats and bloody dogs during the race. Apart from the rain we all had a great day as well as celebrating that night with the winnings. I spent most of the time holding up a broom, with the rest of the time at the Hole in the Wall pub, I think that's the right name. 'The Hole in the Wall' stems from the fact that when one is standing at the bar one can see into the men's loo. It was funny at the time.

The other most memorable time was when I was asked to extend my 13 days to 17. This was to drive a truck for a sea cadet camp at Fort Direction in Southern Tasmania. Mind you nothing exciting happened there other than to say I felt that we were at times treated like the kids they had there for the camp, but it was here in May 1970 that I would meet Ron Holmes. The friendship has stayed to this day as we both have a lot in common and we both served on *HMAS Melbourne* at varying times. It was a very busy 17 days for both myself and Ron, the other driver, who was an ex-stoker who had done more than his share of time on the *Melbourne* as well as time spent at *HMAS Albatross*. Up to the time of writing this book I have had a lot of contact with Ron, who has committed himself to helping his fellow veterans with no reward sought for his work, just the pleasure of doing it. I served with the Naval Reserve until 1976.

My father encouraged me to buy a property of my own in late 1968, when I started to settle down again, so I set about to buy a 27-acre block that belonged to my grandfather. Nothing flash mind you, but it was a start for me.

I still had a few dollars to my name so I set about also buying some machinery as well as a tractor and started working the land. At this time my father had struck up a partnership with a family friend to grow vegetables and to supply the market within the Hydro Electric villages. His partner was having the problem of maintaining his own permanent job as well as keeping the partnership in place. Sadly, the partnership fell through and Dad asked me to fill the void.

It was at this time we needed to update the truck as well as a new tractor and there went the remainder of our funds.

Christmas festivities were out of the question as we in effect had no money till the New Year when we started harvesting our main crops, potatoes, lettuce etc. February soon arrived and I was required to do my agreed 13 days training in the Emergency Reserve and that meant that this time I would be going to New South Wales to do it.

It was a bit of a joke really because when I got to *HMAS Albatross* there was no place for me. I spent most of my time at the swimming pool during the day occasionally looking after a class of new recruits. The best part about it was that I got to meet up with a few of the blokes I had joined up with. There is one thing that has remained in my mind of that period though. There was a group of blokes training for a tour of Vietnam as both ground and air crew for Helicopter Squadron. Some were of my era. Had I re-enlisted, I would have had a very strong chance of being one of those blokes.

It was a Sunday morning in 1971 when I was recovering from 'the night before' and not feeling too well at all. I had severe abdominal pains and difficulty passing water. I really thought it was a result of the previous night from the beer. Dad took me to several medicos but I came away feeling the same, then someone recommended the doctor at Maydena. As soon as I walked in the door he said, 'I know what is wrong with you, you have a kidney stone.' He then advised me to go straight to the Royal Hobart Hospital.

I was admitted and had an emergency IVP with the obstruction relieving itself during the examination. I was discharged 2 days later. I was back to the hospital the next day with similar pains and had another emergency IVP, this time removing a stone. Follow-up x-rays showed other problems. Cysts showed up on my right kidney but at that time I was advised that there was nothing to worry about. I was to find out many years later that was not to be the case. I would end up having a great deal of pain as well as losing my right kidney.

Dad and I got the OK from the Hydro Electric Commission to sell our vegetables in the Strathgordon Village, which at that time was just starting to build up the housing for the married workers. Back in 1968, a 44-gallon drum of Super petrol was worth $16.81 and a 44-gallon drum of diesel was worth $8.86, now petrol at the bowser would be about $180 for a 44-gallon drum.

Our workload continued to increase and as luck happened my younger brother bought a property just down the road and his farm lent itself to growing some vegetables as well. Around this time there was a young man who was going steady with my youngest sister. He was a very keen game shooter and one day we were in the process of harvesting potatoes when he paid us a visit. He casually walked down to the neighbour's dam and spotted some ducks. Afterwards he crept down with his shotgun and took 3 or 4 shots. He came walking up to us with several dead ducks in his hands and with a smile on his face, Dad took one quick look then gave a really big grin.

They were domestic ducks, and to top it off they belonged to someone who would not take the incident lightly. The big smile he had on his face quickly disappeared when both these facts were conveyed to him. He went away with the intention of plucking them so his father would not know that they were of the domestic variety. We took great delight in conveying to him this mistake also. Tame duck and wild duck have different coloured meat and cook differently also! His father would have noticed straight away once they dressed the birds. It certainly was not his day, but I must say his heart was always in the right place.

During this period we had a considerable amount of land that was either fallow or was only good for grass. We ended up buying a herd of young heifers and a purebred Hereford bull to mate with them. When the calves began to drop we hoped that there was a reasonable profit to be made from them. At the beginning we were of the opinion that we had paid too much for them, but we were proved wrong of course.

Chapter 10

My Itchy Feet.

The Hydro Electric village at Strathgordon continued to grow. Here we focused on the retail side but as time went by, it wasn't hard to see that wholesale was the way to go. Mainly for workload reasons we branched out a bit with sales in Hobart and a couple of other outlets, together with the cookhouse at Strathgordon. On reflection, it was this expansion that began to wear both of us down. They were long days, up to 14 hours, sometimes longer, especially when we had to irrigate. It was even difficult to find any time for a quiet beer.

It was during the latter part of 1970 that I received notice that I had a registered parcel to collect at the local post office. Lo and behold it was a medal! The General Service Medal 'Malay Peninsula'. I must say I found it very strange as there was no letter with it. They must have been saving paper at that time! I put it in my bedside drawer at home and forgot about it.

The price of potatoes was always variable but other vegetables were pretty well set. Lettuces were 10 or 15 cents, cabbage and cauliflower 30 cents. We had one patch of cauliflowers just about ready to harvest and along came a big frost and they were no more. It was about this time that we decided it was time to scale down and Dad started talking of pulling out and retiring, so in early 1973 we started to taper off everything. Dad decided that he would sell the farm and retire altogether. We set everything up for a clearance sale and Dad sold his farm sadly under-priced. I tried to sell my small property but had no takers at the clearance sale, so I advertised it and sold it easily. I have regretted it ever since.

I have to admit that I had been somewhat unsettled for quite some time, everything still felt different even though I had been out of the Navy for a few years. I had not had a holiday for so long so I decided to go and visit the South Pacific on a cruise ship.

That was during the fuel oil crisis in 1973. I flew to Sydney to catch the ship there. We went to Tonga, Fiji and New Zealand then back to Sydney. I drank plenty of beer and ate like there was no tomorrow. I suppose the best thing that came out of it was I made some new friends and have kept them till this day.

When I got back home I still had no job. I happened to run into Trevor Chatterton whilst I was in Hobart and he suggested to me that I should try Devonport, suggesting a couple of places I should have a go at for a job. I ended up getting one at Vecon, an onion-packing factory and as it happened the owner was an ex-Navy man.

I checked into Trevor's place for a couple of days until I eventually got into a boarding house in Devonport; from memory it cost me $17.00 a week with meals. When I wasn't working, I called into the pub on the way home so I was always late for my night meals. I found the system of having to be on time for meals so early a bit hard to take and started looking for a house of my own to purchase. It took several weeks, but I found something close to the Devonport area and made the big step for $16,500-00. I now owned a house! It seemed a lot of money in 1974 but it was worth it. I spent the last night before taking over the house in a hotel, mainly because the landlady gave me a bit of a hard time. She thought that I was married and that was why I was buying a house!

The next thing I knew my mother wanted to shift in with my father of course; that happened pretty quickly. The onion season was at its end by this time and I was asked by the boss to supervise the harvesting of the brussel sprouts and of course I took on the job with gusto. It presented me with a few problems, the main one being the chain of command. A case of too many chiefs and not enough Indians, and each had their own way of doing things!

I was the supervisor and I was also picking. I had one bloke in the team that would do a shift in a bakehouse during the night then after a couple of hours sleep, go out with us in the paddock. It was not too long before I began to buckle, the company had a young bloke overall in charge of the paddocks and I have to say his attitude was somewhat domineering and it did not take long for us to come to a verbal stoush. His biggest problem was that he had no idea how to talk to his staff. In the end, I walked. I gave him a minute's notice and went home, angry of course but never the less I didn't want to go back to that.

I had a job offered to me straight away packing vegetables, nothing flash mind you, but it was a job. It was bloody hard work and the money was only basic but it kept the money coming in. It didn't last all that long as I was set the task of stacking and packing off 2 machines, which when full, there was no way I could keep up. I asked the owner for someone to assist me. After a couple of weeks, a young kid, about 16 years old who always had 2 jumpers and a coat on his back set about helping me. He never even took his coat off. It didn't take me long to make up my mind, I gave the boss a week's notice and his only comment was, 'Have you got another job to go to?' My answer was, 'No.' I still had a few bob set aside.

It was around this time of my life that I suppose my attitude to the opposite sex began to mellow because I was introduced to the woman that in the coming years would shape my life in so many ways. There were 3 of us, myself, Barry Flanagan and Noel Brady and we had a routine of going out of a Friday night for a few beers. Starting off at the RSL, we'd then catch the last ferry across the river and quite often hold the bar up at the Edgewater Hotel till stumps. Sometimes that was quite an ordeal in itself.

Chapter 10

I was unemployed for some 3 or 4 months when a job came up at the carpet factory in East Devonport, packing and doing quality control as required. To me it was not the job I wanted for the rest of my life, but it paid the bills. The crew I had with me were fairly left-wing in their views and mine was centre of the right. It was not long before I would receive an ear bashing due to my political views. It was all in good fun though!

The woman that had my attention at this time for all that I knew didn't reciprocate. Then one day Wendy, her daughter, mentioned to me that her mother would like to see me. We arranged a date and from there on a close relationship soon developed. At this time, my folks were away touring the mainland in their camper van and when they arrived back I was no longer a resident at the house. I had moved in with Mary and my parents took possession of my house! During this time, a position came up for a refrigeration defroster at the Edgell factory, so I applied for it and as luck would have it, I got the job.

It turned out the leading hand, Doug, was an astute fly fisherman, one thing that I had always wanted to do. He gave me some lessons. As I would find out though, this job had its drawbacks, during the harvesting season we worked 7 days a week and during the off season I had to come in and defrost the freezer rooms. The money was pretty good so I hung around. At about this time, I approached the local RSL with regards to membership and at first I was told in no uncertain terms that I was not eligible. I did not leave it at that so went back the next week and after considerable robust discussion I was granted membership.

The strange thing about it all was that when I went to purchase the home when I first came to Devonport, I was knocked back for a War Service home loan. It was very strange indeed.

Some people make some stupid and poorly sorted out decisions in their life and I was about to make one of those. It was 1976 and I was approached by a person, an acquaintance, to go into shares with him in a garage, and of course I jumped in. It was not to be a very long business association especially when the bank became involved. The following year I learnt some hard lessons in life. The debt that had accumulated was too much. I was placed in a position where I would in the coming years question my financial status many times. It's here where an old proverb comes to mind, 'An honourable man is at a disadvantage in the world of finance'.

My ex-partner was nowhere to be seen and it seemed I was the bunny. The next few weeks were to be fairly dramatic. I faced my creditors and the Government bureaucrats, one of whom threatened to take everything, including my parents share in the house. Luckily this did not happen and my parents bought my share of the house from me. I have to say here that those people treated me very poorly and my parting words to that Department cannot be put to print.

The next job I found was a builders' labourer for Gordon Ibbott. It was hard work but that didn't faze me. Sadly it did not last that long as at that time the building industry was in a big slump, but it is here that I have to say that Gordon treated everyone the same. Each day during my 6 weeks of employment with him he would come around to the site and say, 'Good day' to each of his crew, then came the day that he had to put some 30-odd men off because there was no work. He approached me in his suit, in the mud, and told me that I was to finish that day. I have great admiration for the man as he did the dirty job himself, not sending someone else to do it for him.

Back in November 1975, I met a man that would be an inspiration to me and a pillar of support in those trying months. He was the late Maurice Kelly. It was the Federal Election dand Maurice was handing out leaflets for the Labor Party and I was doing the same for the Liberals. Our meeting each other that day bought out similar things in each of our lives. We both had served in the RAN and both liked a beer or 2 as well as a good yarn and it was while I was having a beer with Maurice on that Friday evening that I received a phone call out of the blue to say that I had a job waiting for me at Ceilcote. It was a place where they manufactured fibreglass equipment, an international company based here in Devonport. I started there on the following Monday morning, somewhat shocked at the working conditions, but being a little wiser at this time in my life, I tried to avoid the worst where I could.

The company secured a major contract at the Burnie Paper Mills so I volunteered to go. The money was very good, as well as getting $20.00 a day living-away-from-home allowance. My youngest brother, Darrell was working on the same job so we got ourselves a flat for $80.00 a week and we were pretty well-off. Overtime was always there. This was in the late 70s and things were looking up. Getting the experience in the fibreglass industry, especially on construction sites, was one of the best moves for me.

Ceilcote was a very diverse fibreglass manufacturer in its own right, and being able to work for them on the many sites around the country was to my advantage. It also helped me move up the ladder of promotion. Many years later it was made known to me that there was a trade certificate available for those who worked 10 years or more in the industry. All you had to do was provide the details of who you worked for and when for TAFE, and they would organise it, all you had to do was collect it! If only I had known this at the time.

At a couple of hours' notice, 3 of us were sent out to the local paper mill at Wesley Vale to do some pipe work during a 24 hour shut down. Only several hours into the job, I was taken ill and sought out the first aid post and was told to take 2 Aspros and have a rest. I was not happy with that diagnosis and asked the first aid lady to ring my doctor and then drove myself to his surgery. After a brief examination, he put me on the bed and rang the ambulance. I spent the next 5 days in ICU and some 4 weeks off on sick leave. This is when I found out that I had a heart problem. Up to this point I had been a heavy smoker, at times 60 to 80 smokes a day. My doctor's way of changing my smoking habits was up-front. Give the smokes away or be certain of a short life. I did take his advice, thankfully.

Chapter 10

One of the main benefits I found with working away on construction sites was being out in the open, not inside, which was something that bothered me quite a bit. Of course the biggest disadvantage was that I was away from home a great deal, but we coped with that.

My first construction role promotion was for a job at the Risdon phosphate works in Hobart. It was over a period of some 5 or 6 months, travelling home for the weekends. The following year I was asked to go to the Ranger Uranium Mine in the Northern Territory as a worker with a crew of 6, and of course I jumped at the chance, as it was also the type of work that I had not done before.

One of the men, Lorry Thompson, was a bit of a loner and carried a chip on his shoulder most of the time. From the time we left Devonport he proceeded to give me a hard time. He was about 6 feet 2 in. and I stood at 5ft 8in. He always thought that he had an easy victory with me, at least I let him think that. We had been working 12 hour days, 7 days a week trying to catch up on our work as well as trying to finish before the wet season. Bob, our supervisor, decided that we should have the Sunday afternoon off and take some cans of beer and look around the area while we had the chance.

My antagonist was in the truck with me as well as one other. I could smell trouble looming and I was spot-on. I made sure that I drank very little that afternoon, and considering the abuse that I was getting from him, I knew that it would be full-on at some time in the afternoon. As it happened I was the driver of the truck that afternoon and when the time came that I could no longer take his abuse, I stopped the truck, asked him to get out. When he got out I threw 2 or 3 punches and he hit the ground hard. All the while he was still abusing me! I asked him several times to get back in the truck, he refused, so I drove off, leaving him to ponder his position. We were a good hour's drive from the work site in rough country with civilisation a long way away.

It was dark when we got back, and of course I had to report it to security and the police. Considering the area that he was in, the police sent out a team with a blacktracker to find him; he arrived back on-site next morning and for his troubles he was sent home. After that I had a reputation that several wanted to test. This was something that I avoided where I could.

After we were there for some 6 weeks the company would fly us home for a weekend. It would take all day on the Friday to get home and all day on the Monday to get back to the worksite. As the workload began to slow down, the workforce was cut down to only just the boss and me.

On completion, we were sent to Katherine to line out underground tanks in a water treatment plant. By this time I was really getting a liking for the top end; the climate was great. We could not finish the job so Bob the boss, went back to Sydney and I went home to Devonport. I was only home for a short while and was asked to go back to Katherine to complete the job. I went on my own, in the main to test the material and when that proved OK I sent for 2 extra crew members and we completed the job on time.

I had been back in the factory for only a short time when I was again asked to go to Brisbane to get a job started, it was on Gibson Island. I had to fly to Sydney first then there would be 2 of us to go by road from there. The job was to reinstate a pipeline under the Brisbane River that carried phosphoric acid. It had for an unknown reason blown out and caused a big spill. Both of us spent some 2 weeks setting up jigs to get it up and start putting it back together. Our own engineer called on us and gave me the task to supervise the job till it was completed.

There was a four-inch fibreglass pipe inside a six-inch fibreglass pipe and this was inside a ten-inch steel pipe. Both fibreglass pipes were pulled out from under the Brisbane River and laid out in the paddock adjacent to the river. Our job was to cut out all the joints in the fibreglass pipe and re-join it all up and put them back inside the steel pipe. There were 10 in the crew and it took us 10 weeks to put it all back together. It was the hardest job I've ever had. The engineer in Brisbane kept slowing us down, saying, 'You can't do this or that', or 'That's against the rules' and was always underfoot. I was pleased to get out of the place.

One of the jobs I was asked to take on was in Hobart at the zinc works. I was given a utility to take down as a work vehicle. My brother, Darrell and I were to go to Boyer newsprint mill for a couple of days to repair a fibreglass tank. It was not much of a day outside where the tank was standing, so we decided to finish work and go and do some shopping in Hobart. On the way to Hobart on the old highway at the top of Ten Mile Hill, children were waiting to catch their bus home after school and as we approached the area, one child was chasing another and ran out in front of us. His head made an indentation into the windscreen in front of Darrell on the passenger side. Luckily I was only travelling slowly.

We stopped immediately, with adults running to help the young boy, a doctor was there in some 2 minutes, police and ambulance followed. The police sergeant gave an instruction to his junior officer to lock me up and take our work ute away for inspection, but was told by the young constable that the witnesses said it was clearly not my fault and he relented.

This really shook me up, an innocent young life almost taken. It brought back memories from July 1979 when I was given the bad news that my young nephew had been killed after getting off his school bus. Alas he had crossed the road from behind the bus. It had been a big loss to us all. The boy who had run out in front of us was taken to hospital with head injuries. I rang our work office in Devonport and they put me in touch with legal representation in Hobart. I was given instructions not to make a statement to the police. I did however, because the police kept at me. Sometime later I received a letter from the police department absolving me of all blame and told me that the youth had recovered from his injuries.

1985 was my busiest year in the job, as well as having its own dramatic period for me. My job took me to a gold mine near Tenant Creek, from there to South Australia, then back to Melbourne. I criss-crossed the country 4 or 5 times. At one time I was in Melbourne helping the Melbourne crew out. I had to go to the Tullamarine Airport to pick up 2 more of the crew who were sent over to help us out. Whilst driving back on the freeway I had an accident.

The ute I was driving ended up in the back of a car: both were undrivable. It turned out the ute I was driving was not even registered. It was not the nicest way to find out. When the police found out they were at first under the impression that I had stolen it until they did a check with my boss. I was not feeling the best. The accident had shaken me up a bit. I visited the local doctor and under his instructions I packed my bags and went home to Devonport.

I again went back to Port Pirie and not only had some problems with getting material to complete the job but also had the same problems with labour as well. My troubles were of a mixed bag. I wasn't getting much cooperation from management at the home office and was told some years down the track that someone wanted my job, and to get it they sought to make my work look poor.

Chapter 11

The Employment Roundabout.

When I got back I had let things stew a fair bit and handed in my notice as a supervisor and went back on the factory floor. I began to have some back problems and this problem handicapped me in my work. I was put on light duties for about 12 months together with sick leave. I got to the stage where I could not handle it any longer and in 1987 I resigned my employment at Transfield, (Transfield had taken over Ceilcote some 5 years previously). As it happened I had been in that same employment for 10 years so I had pro-rata long service leave and of course I had to take the penalty that went with leaving any employment, basically time on the dole.

This was something that has never sat well with me; it was

the way I was brought up. I was not handling life too well at this point either. I was my own worst enemy. I have always found it difficult to show lots of my feelings or for that matter to talk about them. One of the big mistakes that I have made was that I took up an offer of employment with a local small business, the owner of which I had known for most of my life. It was to be another of those hard lessons in life – business and friendship don't always mix! From the first day there was a problem and I felt, though he may not have agreed, that I would make the perfect salesman. As history says, I didn't make the grade. I wonder how many tried after me. I lasted about 4 and a half months. Well I was back in the dole queue again applying for anything and everything that was around. I went to night school and did a boiler attendant's course but as I was to find out, that was like chasing fairies at the bottom of the garden as all boilers were being made automatic.

A job was advertised for a shift foreman at an onion-packing factory, so I applied. After several interviews I was given the job. I started there on the 16th January. It was 1989 and the packing season started that week. I was thrown in as it all started. I must say that I had a very good opposite number on the other shift, as he was a great help for the first few shifts. It was about this time that I had my first operation on my throat. It turned out to be a thyroid problem.

For me as shift foreman, my starting time was usually some 2 hours before the main shift, whether it was the day or night shift. The packing season was usually about 4 and a half months with part-time day shift packing as required. At other times we would pack potatoes for the mainland market. The place was very busy most of the time and holidays were fitted in where possible. During one very frosty morning I started to set up the machinery for the day's packing of potatoes. I set the machinery running and went around to clear the belts, a mistake, my hands were very cold and while clearing the belts I lost the tip off my forefinger; because my hands were so cold I did not feel it for some minutes, only realising when I noticed the blood. Six weeks off work resulted.

It was on the 17th of March 1989 that I was told that we had lost my mate Maurice; he had drowned while diving at Granville Harbour. I was shocked and angry as these things are not supposed to happen to your mates. We had enjoyed a great friendship and memories are sharp, even today. I often think of him, he would quite often phone up and ask, 'your place or mine for a beer?'

During August of the same year, I was having a few beers with a few of the blokes at the RSL. One made mention that we both had entitlements to pensions with the Department of Veterans' Affairs for our service. He served on *HMAS Sydney* and me on *HMAS Melbourne*. At that time the department was visiting the various centres giving interviews regarding pensions etc. It turned out that, as a result of correspondence with the Department of Defence, I had 3 days of 'operational service' arriving out of my Vietnam Service.

Since arriving in Devonport early in 1974, I had been an active member in the local branch of the Naval Association, attending meetings and being active in the Association's activities which were many. But I cannot recall having been told of any notification to me or for that matter any other person that served in Logistic Support during the Vietnam conflict, in regards to the 'Beazley Instrument' as to having an entitlement for a disability pension and all that went with it. This was signed and took effect from the 22nd of May 1986. As I have mentioned previously, I cannot recall this document or rather a copy of it ever being tabled at any meeting.

Armed with the bit of information that I had received from the brief visit to the DVA, I sent to Canberra for copies of my service records and of course a copy also of my service medical records. It turned out to be very much a surprise and some of it is having severe impact on my health to this day. I had often been in a position where I have had to question my own health issues on any given day unknowingly unaware of their sources, but here it was in black and white. After listening to other veterans I sought out the pension's officer at the Devonport RSL for some help in making a claim on hearing loss.

When I showed him my documentation he withdrew any offer of help and only suggested that I make a claim through the Defence Department. I soon reached the conclusion that he was not interested in the hard ones. At this point in time an Army Sergeant joined our circle, he was an ex-Vietnam 9 RAR and served in Vietnam in 1968-69. He encouraged me to join the local branch of the Vietnam Veterans. From this association I gained a great deal, in friendship as well as valuable information.

Things moved along at my work place but there was some

tension in the camp as there had been a change of foreman on the other shift and at times his attitude was not as it should have been. During the season of 1991 which is January to May my hold on my position of employment was at best very weak and on the 3rd of May the same year, my employment was terminated. I have to say I was at best, very distressed. I suppose I was my own worst enemy in many ways.

I will stand tall on the issue of having a very good relationship with those employees that had worked on my shift. I made a pact with myself that I had to be fair to all and that included my employer. There had been some employees that didn't last many days before I showed them the door, but those that put their best foot forward were told of my appreciation. So much so that on the day of my dismissal they all wanted to go out on strike and of course I could not be a party to that. With notice from the manager, I decided to give him pointers of what had been going on within his factory. I had previously told the factory floor manager of drugs being distributed within the workplace, but no action had been taken by anyone and I found out that my comments had not been passed on to the general manager. This lack of communication in the management does convey poor leadership, however I was still dismissed.

I got home that day feeling as if the whole world was against me. I was only 50 years of age and with little hope of gaining employment anywhere else. Over that weekend I made up my mind that I would put in for a service pension with Veterans' Affairs.

My doctor had been treating me for some years and when I took the medical report to him he was thoroughly helpful. My doctor, Dr. Anthony Blake, has always been a compassionate man in all the time that I have known him. As well as being a Second World War veteran himself, he supports those that have served with that same compassion.

From there I went home and basically waited for the mail. This action as I was soon to find out was probably the worst thing that one can do. I would sit in a chair and stew and on each day that there was no mail, I would get angrier.

On the 7th of June 1991 I underwent surgery to have a mass removed from my right nostril for the second time. By this time it was a worry to me and of course the surgeon did not help either. He made mention that 'Agent Orange' may be the cause. I'm afraid I will have to let history judge that for me.

It is at this point that Mary came into her own. Up to this point I had always tried to keep Mary in the background of some of my life, public to those close to me but very private to the outside world so to speak. This attitude to some may seem strange but it was the way I needed it to be.

Mary was my rock many, many times. She has no naval background and while this does make it a bit harder to relate my naval experiences to her, I have to say that Mary has supported me though, through thick and thin and has never wavered on any issue. That's what makes our relationship very solid.

I am not sure if I was naïve or a bit slow on the uptake, but I never sought a copy of my medical files from the Defence

Department till May 1991. It did make it that bit harder to seek a disability pension from DVA. I turned out to be a bit of a Pandora's box, as I had very little knowledge of half of what it contained and the seriousness of some of its contents.

A couple of months after I had put my application in for a service pension, Veterans' Affairs sent me a letter refusing that same application and telling me if I wanted to appeal, to follow their instructions. This I did and after some 5 months I was granted a service pension in September 1991. I was very pleased to see the back of those bloody dole forms and all the bull that goes with them. It was mentioned to me that an ex-Navy bloke was assisting veterans with their pension claims, his name was Ian Hardy. (We were to lose him as a result of cancer some time ago.) My first meeting with him took 5 hours; we had quite a bit in common. He was an inspiration to many and a bit of a pain in the butt to some of the delegates at Veterans' Affairs – a good bloke!

Veterans' Affairs sent me to a psychiatrist in relation to my service pension application and he could not find any psychological or psychiatric illness which would incapacitate me. However during my association with Ian Hardy at one point he strongly suggested to me that I should make a claim for Post-Traumatic Stress Disorder. I have to say that this was not something that I could relate to in any way, as I did not have a clue what he was talking about. He rang the psychiatrist himself and made an appointment for me and eventually his diagnosis was as follows:

> *I interviewed Mr. Browning at my rooms on the 5/11/92. He has a post- traumatic stress disorder associated with war experiences and this is producing a significant reactive depression. The outlook for this is still uncertain, but there may be some doubt as to whether he will ever be able to resume full-time employment.*

Some years later I would again face this problem. I was having considerable problems with my own personality, but I didn't know what the problem was.

PTSD does creep up on you, as it did to me and the problem was it had ongoing connotations. I first of all have to be honest with myself and fill in some of those gaps or in this case what tricks PTSD will play with your mind. Here is the one I now dread and that is suicide. This is the first time I bought this to the surface, mainly because I can now face the thought, though with some distaste. I had for a long time let this flow through my every day thoughts and it gradually built up from there. I rang the Vietnam Veterans counselling service and had an appointment made to see John De Jong. Counselling took place twice weekly for a start, and then with progress being made, it was moved to once a week. In a letter to my GP, John De Jong set out the diagnosis as depression, anxiety and stress with post-traumatic amnesia. There were several major incidents that were the catalyst and one I have described earlier of the death of John Hutchinson

I do clearly remember the next fatality which happened in the Sulu Sea while patrolling in that area on our way to South

Vietnam and meeting up with HMAS *Sydney* and escorts. My usual place of duty during flying operations at this time was in the Aircraft Control Room, but because of my previous experience on the mirror platform I was asked to fill in. That was no problem. My duty on the mirror platform was to check aircraft during their final approach for landing, and the check was through binoculars to make sure the aircraft flaps were in the right position and the hook was in the down position, whilst also checking for anything out of place.

While the aircraft in question made its final approach, I checked and passed the message visually with a thumbs-up. When the aircraft touched down on the flight deck, its hook hit the wire but the knuckle broke that holds the wire together. The Mirror Officer was shouting into his mike for the pilot to pick the revs up, as was I. Sadly, over those next few seconds the pilot ejected but the observer did not and the aircraft crashed into the sea over the angle deck.

I raced up the deck, looked down and could see him with his face forward, he still appeared to be in his seat and then sank into the sea. It's still all very real to this day, but I am managing to live much better with it.

One thing that needs mentioning here is that we were always encouraged to look after our mates and in this case the aircrew were shipmates. It was also within my role as flight-deck aircraft handler to keep lives safe whenever or wherever possible, and I have always seen this incident as having failed in my role.

I have to say that the sessions have helped me immensely.

John talked me through all of the events that had tormented me for all this time and made it easier as we progressed through the sessions. John did suggest medication to me and at first I was quite reluctant, but when he explained to me that there were big changes from the medication that I had taken before I agreed.

One other subject that is very pertinent in this was my drinking. I would have several stubbies then have a few glasses of red and this mixed with other medications for my various health problems was not a very good mix at all.

There can be various conclusions drawn from this statement and it was one that would lead me to an Administrative Appeals Tribunal, well down the track.

These sort of situations where the people that should know one's full entitlements do very little research on them and because of this make mistakes which take time to remedy.

There was a brief interruption to all of this kafuffle. I had been having a great deal of trouble with my right thyroid. I had had my left one removed some years previously. This time I was told not to waste any time with my decision and get it done ASAP.

Chapter 12

Claims and Counter Claims!

At the same time I was having a great deal of trouble with back problems and started using a walking stick. The radiology report of that time did not paint a very good picture at all, but I suppose the best answer to it all is I am a survivor. It was in the first week of September 1992 that I received some really bad news. Dad had gone into hospital to have a prostate operation, and sadly during the operation he had a severe heart attack. From there it was downhill for him, and on the 5th he passed away. Even now some 20 years later it is hard to realise he has gone. While he was with us he held the family together. With his passing all that hard work had been pushed aside. It saddens me that it's all gone with a huge gap left behind.

During this process I have had reason to write many letters to many people, organisations and of course various government departments. One of the biggest problems that I have had to face is that politicians have, at best, always sat on the fence with no clear answer to the problem or problems that I have put to them. I suppose most of all, I, like many others, have had a great deal of difficulty with the various governments that have sat in Canberra with their various changes to legislation. My motive was always a collective attitude, by this I mean any result that could or would come out of it would hopefully benefit all veterans in general. They may disagree with my comment but if those are their thoughts, why are we having inquiries still to this day?

Early in January 1993 at a meeting with Ian Hardy, Ian expressed concern with regards to my having no 'operational service' for my service in the Malay Peninsula area in 1965 and his suggestion was that we should make contact with the British High Commission in Canberra. After a phone call I wrote a letter to the liaison officer, in fact I wrote again on the 15th March with the response that the Ministry of Defence is only a small department and gets many enquiries each day. Several weeks later the staff officer, Chief Petty Officer Chris Dunne, sent me a copy of the Defence Council Instructions, which gave the ships, dates and medals information; quite a windfall. This had been released on the 29th of January 1971.

It took them a while to sort it all out. The comment of the Executive Officer who signed for the documents that I received was 'The medal (*Malay Peninsula*) was not easily earned.'

Incidentally there were some 14 Australian warships that

took part in that conflict during 1964/65/66. With all of the information that both Ian and I had gathered and made available to the Department during the process of my claims, there was very little positive response from them.

Over some time now there have been comments from mostly those that have had no naval experience of the Indonesian confrontation and the logistic and escort duties during the Vietnam war. The comments being made were 'you blokes never done anything'. On the surface it does appear so, but I would say that take us out of the equation and the results would probably have been different. Receiving very little response from the Department, I rang the office of the Ombudsman. I put it to him that I had been unreasonably refused a disability pension in respect of my service in the Malay Peninsula Conflict.

By this time I was a very angry man, some of it for very good reasons and some for not the right reasons. The 'very good reasons' were that all this time 'we' had still not been recognised for our service and even a lot of letter writing to politicians on both sides did very little to set the record straight.

The Ombudsman received a letter back from the Department dated the 13/10/93 stating that they would recognise my Malay Peninsula service giving various reasons for the delay in it all.

About this time I was having considerable problems in settling my superannuation payout and it was to end with pretty much a negative result for me. They refused to pay me out in the main because of my service-related disabilities and it was from there that I had to have a lawyer take it on for me. In the end I ended up getting just over what I paid into it. My opinion of insurance companies is not easily put into print.

Another problem had emerged from my records at DVA. On my records it states that I had served some days on *HMAS Sydney* — what a lot of bloody nonsense! It's no wonder Vets go off the rails.

It was not the best year of my life. I have to say that if I hadn't sought some help from the Vietnam Veterans' Counselling Service I would not be here today. Frustration and anger mixed with the grog do not always have a very good ending and I have to say there were several times that I was on the edge.

I find it very difficult here as I write this to put it into words that portrayed my feeling at that time. Dr. Briggs asked me at one of the sessions that I had with him if I ever considered suicide. Yes, I had, but only briefly as it didn't take me long to come to terms with my life and what I can be, in a nutshell, only what I can make it to be.

As I recall he prescribed Sinequan, 2 a day. I found them pretty hard to take in every way. It was some 2 weeks later that he prescribed 3 Sinequan a day. On the 25/2/93 I received a letter from DVA advising that they had determined that my PTSD was caused by my 'operational service' but the assessment was deferred pending further investigation.

It was at this stage that Ian had wisely suggested to me that I should seek some counselling from Helen Spinks.

My mother had sold the house by this time and purchased a small unit in Devonport and at the end of February my brother Anthony and his wife came up from down south to help shift Mother into her new abode.

It was early in April that I received notice via Ian that DVA had given me a 50% disability pension. With the problems I was having with the pills from Dr. Briggs, at my next visit I asked to be taken off them and the combination of these 2 events made me a fair bit happier.

It was at about this time that I got elected to the position of secretary of the local branch of the Vietnam Veterans Association. Here I was in effect put in the position to also raise funds for a memorial barbecue on council land and from there it was a rather big task to write to the various business houses and ask them to put up cash or kind and they did, in a big way. This project would be the best public relations profile that Vietnam veterans could have hoped for.

Darrell Banham and I turned the first sod of dirt, then Darrell took over and did the best job coordinating it all as well as using his 'chippy' tools. While all this was being put together I was still writing letters, as well as knocking on doors for material as well as cash and again I have to say I had very few knock backs.

All this time between Ian and I we were writing to as many politicians as was practical, lobbying for the changes that were long needed in the Veterans Entitlement Act to help all and sundry.

At a session with Helen Spinks, she discussed with me

the many facets of my problems, and myself. To some it may seem that I had lost the plot, maybe I had, but again I have to say that in my life there has been separate parts: my service time, as well as my before and after life. The combination of them all is not always a good mix.

The memorial barbecue and wall were going ahead in leaps and bounds with at times some 30 or more Vietnam veterans and their partners putting their shoulders to the wheel. Dave Moles, the VVAA President, was also busy organising the Dedication for early October, so we all had a deadline to meet.

It was on the 14th of July 1993, that I fronted the AAT hearing in Launceston and it was held over because of a federal court case. It appeared that the work many others and I had put in was bearing fruit at long last. There was a High Court decision to be handed down in Sydney with regards to 'operational service' any day now and we all are waiting with bated breath.

The dedication went off with a bang. There was a very good crowd in attendance, and now there is something in place for the community to use and pause for a moment or 2 and remember the sacrifice that has been made.

Moving some years forward to recent days (2011), a Rotary Club in Devonport set about to commemorate the Tasmanian blokes who died in Vietnam with an avenue of trees adjacent to our memorial wall with concrete plinth and a plaque on top giving details of their deaths in Vietnam. Gerald O'Dea gave the main address because he was the first Tasmanian to be conscripted into the Australian Army. I have to say it was a job well done by all concerned, another way of remembering our fallen. What I did notice is that there were many Viet Vets in attendance and it shows that they still care and are always mindful of their mates.

With the ongoing lobbying of many veterans in respect of what should be veterans' entitlements — especially Navy Veterans, in this endeavour I have met and made many friends Australia wide: Roger De Lisle, Allan Lees, Ron Holmes, Dr. John Carroll and many more.

This in part enabled Navy Veterans who served in the Far East Strategic Reserve to gain true recognition. I received a phone call from DVA requiring me to go to Hobart to be checked out for a GARP test for a Totally and Permanently Incapacitated Pension. This happened after I had received information that I had been granted 135 days 'operational service'. A far better outcome than the original period I had been granted in the early part. This, I would not have received if we had not fought very hard for it, of that I am sure.

The 7th of October 1993 is a date that is set in concrete for me. This month was a very busy time for me as everything that could happen, did happen.

The building of the new RSL club rooms was nearing completion and everything was due to be moved into the new building at the end of October.

The official opening was set for early November 1993. It was a great day for all concerned.

It is also the time that my mother turned me away from her door, never to pass through it ever again. It was a very heavy burden for me to carry, and was so until her passing away in 2009. I did try several times to set it right, but each time I was turned away. On reflection, this was not the first time I had been turned away. Locks had been changed on the home I had purchased not long before I had moved in with Mary, and to this day I am unable to work out the reasons behind that move. I found it very hard to handle, in so many ways. Parents are supposed to be your mentors for all their lives. I had always been very close to both my mother and father but here I was turned away.

This happened at a bad time for me as my health had deteriorated and I was having problems handling life in general.

It was early in 1994 that the results of my last appeal to the Administrative Appeals Tribunal were passed on to me by my legal eagle that had done a great job in representing me. They had lifted me up to 60% with my disability pension.

I had spent the previous Christmas period in Melbourne with Mary and her family and while we were there, our Corgi passed away. It was a sad time as she was so attached to us, as we were to her. We had not been home very long when Mary brought another pup into the household. His name is Peppi.

Chapter 12

Life's Building Programs.

It was during the month of April 1994 that I decided to take part in an Advocate course. I had been helping various Vets with their pension claims. Sadly in retrospect while doing this, I was neglecting my own life in general. It was during this period that I had an appeal being processed in the Department of Veterans' Affairs, receiving confirmation that I had had my pension increased to the intermediate rate forthwith. Here I was still seeing Helen Spinks together with the various doctors, and some days later I was diagnosed with glaucoma.

I had also been having some problems with my throat with a similar problem as before, this being the other half of my thyroid was on the blink, and on the 29th June, 1994 I had that fixed. The surgeon was a very likeable bloke and if one would meet him one would not consider him to be a surgeon and I mean this in the most polite manner.

My life was about to undergo a big change for all the right reasons, Mary and I had decided to get married. The 27th of August 1994 was the big day. It was only a small wedding, just 2 others to witness the good deed. It did make a lot of changes to my life. It gave me an incentive to become motivated and get on with life no matter where it led. With the planning of the wedding, we also had a plan to build onto the house as well as buy it. I applied for a Defence Service Home loan to purchase it and the money I had saved for a 'rainy day' was used for the additions.

I sought 4 quotes for the main building and various quotes for other parts of the internal bits and pieces. For the period of the building program I was in my glee. At one stage, I had some 10 contractors on-site. In the end I had supervised nearly every nail that went into the building.

It brought me back to where I had wanted to be for some time — happy with my life as it was. A very old Chinaman once told me, 'When you get up in the morning wherever you are and look up into the sky and smile, the world is bigger than all of us eh!'

It was a very rewarding time for me, after what seemed a lifetime, everything was on track. My only problem was the builder himself, his price was the best, but his attitude to his work did leave a lot to be desired. However, as it happened all the work was next to finished by Christmas which made it better for us.

Chapter 12

The main building by the contractor was finished in mid-January and I set about putting some of my own finishing touches to the surrounds. All this time I was having continuous contact with the Department of Veteran Affairs, both on my own and also through a legal adviser. Of course, with this came constant contact with various members of the medical fraternity, my own doctor as well as the various medical specialists. For some time now, I had similar kidney problems as in the early 70s.

During the early part of 1995, Mary and I went again to Melbourne to visit the family for a couple of weeks. For some time I had ongoing phone contact with Roger De Lisle. Roger had served in the Navy several years prior to my time and in doing so had served in the Far East Strategic Reserve. Like many other Vets of his time he received very little recognition of his service.

While I was in Melbourne I had the opportunity to meet with Roger as well as Bob Gibbs. I found Roger a very likeable bloke who was very well-versed in the fight for recognition. We sat in the RSL building in Melbourne City and talked, drank coffee and of course I learnt from these 2 blokes. It was early in April that we came back to Devonport and back to reality.

At the end of August I had an ultrasound and an IVP x-ray the following week because the previous one was not clear. I met with my doctor several days later and he confirmed that it was a cyst on my right kidney that was the problem — 4cm in diameter! I had a CT scan and then I went to see the urologist and from the outset I was put at ease; he has a great approach with his patients.

It didn't take him long to act as I was called into St. Vincent's Hospital in Launceston the following week and admitted on the Tuesday, with the following day set down to drain the fluid from my right kidney.

I was placed in the CT scanner and told not to move while they moved the scanner in and out with a large needle being inserted in my back. The closer they got to the cyst the more stressed I became. They had numbed my back but once it got close to the kidney I was subjected to some pain. In all, the job took about an hour. I was allowed to leave hospital the next day and went back to see Rob Jensen the following week for the results and I have to say I was very apprehensive of what he may have to say. It was certainly not what I was looking for. The cyst was bleeding and it would have to be drained again in 3 to 4 months. If that didn't fix the problem it meant major surgery.

To keep my mind off it, I came up with an idea to give the local branch of Vietnam Veterans a lift with their profile, which required me to first get the OK from the Mayor.

It was to have the Mayor present each veteran with a certificate of appreciation from the local council. It was to come to fruition in the near future.

I went to Hobart to go before the Veterans' Review Board on the 22nd November and in effect I should have stayed at home. As from the first time that I went before them, the story was still the same, a lack of knowledge of my naval service.

Chapter 12

With it being so close to the silly season, we set about to get ready for visitors for the Christmas break. Mary's brother and his wife were to be here for several weeks and it was a great time to get away from the hubbub of the past 12 months. We all had a good time.

A friendship had grown in the last few months with Rod Clarke, an ex-digger who was wounded in a fire fight at the battle of 'Balmoral' in Vietnam. It had knocked him around a fair bit but he lived his life fairly full-on and harmed no one in the process. Sadly the friendship did not last, as we were to lose him to an aneurysm. We were in the RSL club rooms about to have a cup of coffee, when he sat on a stool alongside me and then fell on me. I cradled him in my arms till the ambulance arrived. Somehow I knew he would not make it.

It was to be a sad time for all. Rod was buried on Monday, 13th of Jan 1997.

The irony of it was that we had decided he would be nominated for President and I would be nominated for Vice President. Sadly only I would make the voting positive.

It was at this time that my appeal to the Administrative Appeals Tribunal over my disability pension was well underway. The main question being: was I able only to work 8 hours or 20 hours a week? My contention was that I was only able to work no more than 8 hours per week. From there it was up to the various practitioners to put their views forward.

During this time I had to go back to St. Vincent's Hospital to have the cyst drained again and it wasn't a success which meant major surgery. This was something I was not looking for, however late in September 1997 I was admitted to hospital for the Op. I awoke in the high dependency ward not feeling the best at all. To get at my kidney to drain it they had to take a rib out and let me tell you it's not the best loss to wake up to. I was not too well for several days, but I can vouch for the staff at St. Vincent's hospital. They really looked after me, not a thing worried them and they were always eager to pass 5 minutes with you.

I ended up staying for 10 days and it took me quite some time to get back somewhere near myself again.

The best news to cheer me up came several weeks later from my legal rep, Richard Webster. He rang to say that my appeal had come out in my favour, I was granted a T&PI pension. With that news a lot of the pressures that had been on me for some time were lifted.

Now I had to get myself back on my feet in the best way I could. It wasn't long before the kidney problems were at me again, this time I had got out of bed, went to the toilet and all I passed was blood. Not the nicest view at any time. Within several days I had more x-rays and was admitted to hospital again, this time Robert said he would do an exploration operation to see if the kidney could be saved.

After coming out of the recovery ward, Robert spoke to me briefly and told me that he could not reach the cyst, so there was no way the kidney could be saved.

I would spend 7 days with bouts of intense pain and low blood pressure, this was something that I had thought was a part of my kidney problem, but it turned out later that it wasn't.

Chapter 12

My weight began to go down at a fairly fast rate, my date with the coming surgery was only several weeks away and it was a battle now for me to stay on top of it all. During this time I lost about 15 kilos. During that time I found it very hard to stay positive, I was losing my self-esteem as well as my self-confidence. I really thought that I was at the end of the road. I had it in the back of my mind that to lose one kidney would be the end of it all. It was not till some 2 days prior to my operation did I came to terms with it all and I am sure that a big change in my outlook was my saviour.

I was admitted to St. Vincent's Hospital on the 28th of October and scheduled the next day for surgery. I woke up feeling quite the worse for wear and with a lot of tubes and leads going everywhere. Mary and Kerrie were there to see me but I would have to agree I wasn't feeling the best for a conversation.

The intensive care nursing staff were always at their best and they really looked after me. Nothing was a problem to them. I was put on morphine and it did not react with me in the best way. If I recall, at that time we all thought that the morphine was in part the cause of my periods of low blood pressure. Again we were wrong. I spent 7 days in ICU.

I was only out on the main ward for 2 days and Robert Jensen was so pleased with my progress that he said I could go home on the weekend. Probably the best thing that happened to me while recovering was a surprise visit by 2 old mates from my Navy days. There were 2 heads looking from the door, Slim Smith and Leo Kirkman. They were both over in

Tasmania for a holiday. Trevor Chatterton had briefed them on my hospitalisation. We had a long talk as we had a lot to catch up on.

I also had another old mate, again from my Navy days. Geoff Singline called in and I hadn't seen him for some 20 years; what a day! The visitors did not stop there as John and Jennie Pidgeon came to see me the next day, this as well as all the get-well cards together with flowers and other bits and pieces were very well placed to add to the mending of my body. Let's face it, the scar that was left behind at first glance looked like I was almost cut in half. This cut was in the same place as where the rib was taken out. On the 8th of November I was allowed to go home, via my stepdaughter's home, staying there for a day.

Chapter 13

All the Queen's Men

Each day was a bonus and my body was mending very quickly. So good that we decided to trade in our old Toyota Corona and buy a new car, something that had not happened for us for a long time. 1997 finished off with everything being on a positive note.

Christmas was fairly quiet for all of the family. I might add here that I had inherited 5 stepdaughters and 2 stepsons along with all their children, so it had grown to be a very sizeable family, and in a couple of the family branches some great grandchildren. If I was to reflect on my life at this point, my biggest disappointment would be that I had no children of my own, probably no different than a lot of other people, but I never chose to not have kids, sadly it just happened to turn out that way. The bonus of my situation was being a step father to Mary's children and that I have become a part of their lives. At last count there were some 24 grand and 32 great-grandchildren, not forgetting one great-great-granddaughter; it's one big family.

By mid-January I was back into helping out at the RSL club as the gaming coordinator. There was a bit of lethargy in the outlook of several of the executive members but that would be sorted at the coming elections, I hoped!

The election of the new committee was held on the 9th of February, and though I was beaten for the top position, I was elected to the Senior Vice President's position.

I was always in favour of forward thinking in respect of ideas that give better outcomes for all concerned, but I'm afraid that there has been several members that would rather sit back and watch the proceedings until a time comes when they can take the credit; a very selfish outlook. It was on the 1st of May that one of the committee approached me with a complaint regarding someone operating a gaming fixture illegally within the club. Of course being the gaming top jock in the club, I had to act upon that complaint.

The person at the centre of the problem wrote a letter of complaint against me and sought an apology from me! To top it all off, the support and the value of that support I received was as good as the bloke that didn't deliver it. I'm sure those that were about at that time know who I am talking about. During this time I had some discussion with the TAB in regards to a promotion of some kind, and several days later they came up with the idea of having Ricky Ponting come to the club on a set day. This is something I was really pleased about, something like this was good for all concerned or should have been.

On the 25th of May, I continued to get a lot of negatives from those concerned. During this period I took the time to review my health and where I was with it and came to the conclusion that to continue in this present situation was not in the best interest of my wellbeing, and so, here I must quote from my diary: *'After I finished pokies, wrote my resignation out and gave it to the President & left them, my key on the secretary's desk, their problem now.'*

My statement there was a bit mixed up, but that was the way I felt at that time.

It took me a while to come to terms with it all. I have for all my life taken it for granted that people on the whole are supportive of what is right, sadly in this case it should have been more so as all or nearly all did wear a uniform at one time or other and therefore should have been supportive of each other.

Chapter 14.

and Life Goes On.

It was in October 1998 that I decided that I would attend the Fleet Air Arm reunion to celebrate the 50th anniversary of the Fleet Air Arm. I was very pleased that I decided to go. I met a lot of the blokes I had served with and hadn't seen for a long time, some of them since 1966. We had a lot to catch up on. But time went so quickly for all of us and before we knew it, it was time to head home.

What the trip did do was open up correspondence between some of us and in the latter part of 1998, the then President of the local branch of the Vietnam Veterans Association thought it would be a good thing if we could get the members motivated by seeking some assistance from the Department of Veterans' affairs for some funding to get some blokes interested in golf.

This we did, but for myself at this stage I was still using

a walking stick, something I'd done since early 1982. I used this as motive for me to have some physio and try and get off the stick! This was the best move I had made in a long time. Each time the physio worked on me I had to endure quite a deal of pain, as he did not hold back. He had said to me, 'I will get you off the stick but be prepared for some work as it will get a bit tough', and it was bloody tough. After some weeks of physio though, I was able to go without the walking stick, but kept going with the physio to keep things improving.

About this time I had also experienced times where I was not the best, light-headed and at times all puffed out. Early in 1999 it got too much for me and a consultation with my doctor showed my blood pressure was low, 90/60.

Things were not looking good at all. He also did some blood tests but they were not conclusive and he put it down to the eye drops I was using. A week later it was 110/60, not a lot of difference there. But another week later again it appeared to be better at 130/80.

My golf at that time was still pretty rough, but improving slowly. I played my first competition at the Elderslie golf course in a Legacy fund-raiser. This was on the week of Remembrance Day and the day after both Mary and I visited my brother and his wife, staying there for a couple of days. Visiting and fitting a game of golf in as well, made it a very busy week.

Rodney Jordan and I continued to play twice weekly at the Thirlstane golf course, mostly on Mondays and Thursdays and definitely only social.

Chapter 14

It was on the 11th of May that my greatest achievement to that point with golf was realised and that was an eagle on the 8th hole, it's a par 5, 431m. For me, it was a real high, something that will probably never happen again. A couple of years after this, I decided that I needed a change of golf courses and moved to Port Sorell Golf Club. It was a course that I had only played a couple of times on and while the course itself is a little on the dry side, I started to see some improvement in my golf overall.

They too had a 'Veterans' group' (over 60s) and their day was Tuesday each week. The next golf highlight for me was November '06 when I scored a hole in one, on a difficult hole. My prize for winning that was a certificate from the golf club and 6 golf balls.

It was early August when I received the sad news that Toby (my brother-in-law), who had married my eldest sister Joan, had passed away. He would be sorely missed by the family.

Well it was back to Hobart for the Legacy golf day at the Elderslie golf course, for me this course is still giving me lessons as I still cannot come to terms with it. Oh well, it looks like I'll be back here next year to try again.

It was towards the end of the year 2000, in mid-October, that there seemed to be some problems coming out of the RSL that no one seemed to want to talk about it, and it was so hard to get to the bottom of it. It was only later that out of the blue came the news that the treasurer had been sacked. From my knowledge of the Club's constitution that cannot be done. It had to go to a special general meeting of the members. In a nutshell, the members elected the treasurer so they were the only ones that could dismiss the treasurer by voting on that issue. Mary and I left for Melbourne on the 14th of December and on that same night there was a special general meeting that was supposed to sort all the problems out with the 'Hoogland' affair, but it proved to be a real fizzer. At the time I remember feeling that things could only get worse. It did for Pieter Hoogland who, I believe, was given a rough deal all round both by the RSL and the law itself.

Our trip to Melbourne soon came to its conclusion but not before I had got a couple of games of golf in, as well as a couple of fishing trips, which really made it a great trip. We got back several days before my 60th birthday and it was a real milestone for me. It was a great weekend as most of my side of the family turned up.

I went to the local RSL annual general elections and what a fizzer that was. There was no treasurer still in place and very little in the way of new faces that put up for election for the committee.

At this time I continued to have some physio on my neck as well as the lower back and continued to feel better because of it, so much so that I was playing better golf. Not as good as John Pidgeon though, who at the Stanley Legacy golf day in late April topped the day with a hole in one. It was about this time that I put a proposition to the local branch of the Vietnam Veterans Association for a golf day for veterans and their partners state wide and to have it at the Thirlstane,

Chapter 14

with the thought of seeking a grant from the Department of Veterans' Affairs to fund the meals for the day.

After some homework, I put a proposal to Veterans' Affairs for funding and put together a program for the golf day to be held on the 10th of March 2002. Probably the only disappointing part was the roll-up on the day. Only 22 played on the day, all but 2 were locals. We had a barbecue for lunch with a crowd of about 40 who all stayed for the presentations. I had very good support from sponsors around the town, which really topped the day off.

I continued this event when I moved to Port Sorell with some success, though with the first one we had some trouble. The first I knew of it was the week after the competition. A Vietnam Vet really gave me heaps for allowing cheating, apparently a few knew that the winner had cheated. It could have been cleared up sooner if I had been advised at the time, but my response was one of anger and resolve.

I let it be known who the perpetrator was and I have to say I was ready to take a bit of skin off him should he seek to play with us again. I had gathered quite a bit of sponsorship from many of the business houses in and around Devonport. I found it very difficult to front would-be sponsors again and decided I would sponsor future Vietnam Veterans' golf days myself.

It wasn't long before I had problems with my low blood pressure again. This was at the end of April. A reading of 90/60 is not the best and of course I wasn't feeling too flash either. My GP did a blood test which showed a couple of negatives, so he asked me to come back in 2 weeks for another check and again it was down. I sought a referral to see the urologist again, trying to find some answers there. I continued to go around in circles eventually getting to see a specialist at the Latrobe Hospital. Part of the outcome of that was to have an echocardiogram. This did bear the results that I had for so long been looking for.

The diagnosis was detailed as I was told that I had a leaking valve in my heart. I was put on some tablets with the view that this would be the first move to trying to resolve the problem. I was told that the end result may well end up being open-heart surgery.

After all of the toing and froing, it all linked up to the heart problems that I had in my first few weeks in the Navy. I was scheduled to go back for more tests early in the New Year with the hope that the tablets that I was given would resolve the problem. Sadly, bad news seemed to follow bad news with Mary's mother passing away on the 30th June and with me not feeling all that flash, she had to go to Melbourne on her own for the funeral. A great lady, all the time I knew her she treated me as one of the family and for me that was something very special.

It was only a matter of some 2 days and the community had also lost 2 of their World War II veterans, both of whom I had a close friendship with, the late Aub Steers and Stan Jackson.

One of the greatest lessons that I have learnt during my life is that life must go on and one must continue to build on the results of all that comes before you!

Chapter 14

In about 2004, I put pen to paper and did some homework on having a reunion here for aircraft handlers with whom I had served in the Fleet Air Arm. Money was the first thing to put into a work plan, then over several months, I made contact with a few of the mates seeking their thoughts on it. It was a goer, so I sought some financial help from the Department of Veterans' Affairs who looked after me pretty well on this issue.

I looked at many establishments that could cater for the reunion, but some did not fit, one was very blasé about it all. I had approached the Devonport RSL to have our functions there but being their usual pedantic self, they said we could have our functions in the car park underneath the clubrooms, not a very nice setting to welcome interstate visitors at all.

I finally settled on the East Devonport Football club for a barbecue lunch on the first day as a meet-and-greet which went very well with much to eat and drink; the bulk of discussion was on where we had served and with whom. A few jokes went with it of course and again much laughter. It was a good turnout and I must say a lot of the blokes came with their wives and partners. Some that come to mind are Slim Smith, Rod Venning, Trevor Chatterton, Smiley McGowan. The Devonport City Council was very good to us as well, they put on a civic reception for the blokes and their wives, a few speeches were made and a great day was had by all.

The next day was the 24th April and this is a day when all those that served in and around Korea are remembered, it's called Kapyong Day. Two of our blokes were Korean veterans so through various links it was organised for the RSL to run the dedication service with quite a few of our party turning up and giving their support.

The next day, ANZAC Day, we attended the Dawn service at the Devonport cenotaph and had our breakfast at the Gateway Hotel where most were staying.

We then bussed to Ulverstone for the 11 a.m. service and the march. Boags Brewery gave us a barrel of beer, which made the day for all.

Hank Koopman and his wife were also a part of our reunion. Hank and Donna are both accomplished country music entertainers and to cap the day off, Hank presented to all of us a CD of the music. Well done mate, always appreciated.

In 2006, on the 8th June, I made my first submission in regards to May 20th 1963 for *HMAS Melbourne* and its crew and *Supply* and *Yarra* to the then minister assisting the Minister for Defence, the Hon Bruce Billson, with copies to Mr Mark Baker MP for Braddon (2004-2007).

It wasn't until 19th November that I received a response from the Defence Coordination and Public Affairs Department, and it advised me that the government was in caretaker mode. The letter went on to say Minister Billson had asked the Vice Chief of the Defence Force to have a Nature of Service investigate the claim, and was advised that it may not be completed till June 2008.

On the 13th August, I received a letter from Dr. Mike Kelly, Parliamentary Secretary for Defence Support: Dr. Kelly confirmed the HMA ships had travelled through a 'Special Operational Area' but that these waters were declared such for the period of 17th August 1964 to 30th September 1967.

Further, Dr. Kelly stated that special duty requires personnel to be exposed to danger from hostile forces, and he did not accept that there was incurred danger during the transit of Sunda Strait.

Dr. Kelly did leave out some of the detail, seemingly for his own benefit. He mentioned 3rd degree of readiness, but not ABCD Damage Control State of Readiness 2 which was maintained for some 8 hours for the loading and unloading of guns.

For many years, I have been a member of the Fleet Air Arm Association and had attended quite a few of their meetings. At a meeting in Launceston in 2008 the President was retiring, so I put my hand up for election to the position and was voted in and also had to take on the treasurer's job. Because of what I had previously experienced with getting recognition for Korean Vets, I set about trying to find a catalyst for our association and found it with the 60th anniversary of the Fleet Air Arm's involvement in the Korean War. There was vocal support from members but little in the way of physical support, so I set about seeking interested areas like I did with the Aircraft Handlers reunion.

This time I had made up my mind to have the commemorative event based in Launceston. As it turned out the event would be centred on a long weekend which included Easter, which did make it harder to put in place, but if this event meant anything to the individual they would make the effort and attend.

One of the biggest problems was too many lay days, namely Good Friday and Easter Saturday, so what I put in place after making arrangements with Launceston City Council and the Launceston RSL was to have a meet-and-greet on the Thursday. This was held at the All Year Round Hotel and everyone who registered paid a set registration fee with this including a polo shirt, cap, stubby holder and a carry bag.

From there we were given a civic reception by the Launceston City Council where I presented a framed poster to the Lord Mayor and one to Senator Richard Colbeck; the posters were commemorating events of World War II.

Both were accepted with surprise and much appreciation.

Friday and Saturday were lay days, but Sunday, Kapyong Day, was special with the Launceston RSL chairing the ceremony. We had quite a good attendance. The event took about 40 minutes, with one of our visitors laying the wreath.

From there we went to the RSL for lunch.

Next day came to us quickly and I attended Dawn service, which as always tends to bring a tear to my eyes.

At about 10 a.m. we all turned up to march to show the people of Launceston who we were and with 2 of the local Naval cadet unit we fell in at the front of the parade and proceeded to march to the cenotaph, feeling very proud and privileged to be a part of the day.

We then moved to the Launceston RSL club rooms for a convivial or 2, and while the lunch was not what I would call very well-presented, it was a good day. I left the activities at about 4 p.m. feeling a little worse for wear.

At 2 yearly intervals from 1992, I had been having a medical and x-rays to check for symptoms of asbestosis. There was the normal chest x-ray and a consultation with their appointed doctor. These check-ups carried through to the last one in mid-2001, when I received a diagnosis of benign asbestos pleural disease.

Then the specialist went on to say that there is an increased risk for development of a bronchogenic carcinoma (as a consequence of my past tobacco smoking and asbestos exposure) and for the development of a mesothelioma (from my past exposure to asbestos). So far so good!

Consequently, I placed a claim for compensation with COMCARE through the Department of Defence to see if my health problem had credibility. They gave me a yes to my claim, but considering the present diagnosis I have let the claim lapse. At one of my visits to the lung specialist he said to me in very plain English that it was only a matter of time for it to catch up with me owing to my access if you like to the dreaded stuff (tobacco).

I have continued to have check-ups with Dr. Markos in Launceston every 2 years and in 2010 the lawyers acting on my behalf for a civil claim sent my last CT scan to Dr. Slaughter in Brisbane for a review. He suggested that I have another CT scan which related to the previous unclear diagnosis. Recently I sought a lung function test through my GP and it did not come up with a very good result, and from that he has put me on Ventolin to help my daily breathing, with the present diagnosis as plural plaque of both lungs.

For some years there was a concerted effort for research to gather information in regards to Agent Orange and, as it turns out, Agent Blue on the results so far also has a lot to answer for.

I have been a member of the *HMAS Sydney* and Vietnam Logistic Support Veterans' Association for some 10 years or more and I would have to say that as far as an ex-service organisation go they have been at the forefront in pushing the cause of its members. There has been a concerted effort to push for investigation of the 'DIOXIN' scenario; in this case Agent Orange and Agent Blue.

The Naval veterans who were afloat off the coast of Vietnam became subject to the results of the spraying of these dioxins on shore and there have been some estimates of there being something like 19 million tons of them sprayed.

Heavy rainfall, which in Vietnam was often every day, would give a degree of runoff of water (and consequently the dioxins in it) to creeks and on into the river system. From there the flow of water would carry the dioxins to the estuarine waters of Vietnam and out into the sea.

Perhaps I should explain the working of a ship's distillation process:

> *The seawater enters through the underwater inlet and is pumped to the distiller (condenser) and from there to the evaporator. Two coils lay flat on the bottom of the*

evaporator through which passes super-heated steam which boils the seawater.

The seawater rises as steam to the distiller where the steam passes through a nest of copper pipes and is condensed by the seawater circulating around the copper pipes.

A solution of salt and seawater (brine) from the evaporator is pumped back into the sea.

The steam once it has condensed is then pumped to the tanks for which it has been made.

Feed water for the boilers is pure and is not suitable for human consumption whereas the water for drinking, cooking etc. has impurities. The purpose of the electric salinometer is to measure the purity of the water, it can do this because pure water will not conduct electricity, and the low voltage electricity is conducted by the impurities contained within the water. The test cock allows a sample of water to be taken and tested with silver nitrate, which reacts with the chlorine content of the water.

Again I would suggest that those who seek to investigate these matters should make contact with the Dept. of Veterans Affairs, or a Vietnam Veterans' organisation.

From the findings of the study that has been undertaken they found that the distillation of water does not remove but rather enriches certain contaminates, in this case Agent Orange and Agent Blue. In a nutshell, all that served on any of the ships may be subject to some more research into their ongoing problems.

After some brief but very relevant mail from the *HMAS Sydney* Association I sought a copy of the report from a local politician and found that although it was well advanced in its findings so far, it still has a lot to do yet to give a proper outcome that is relevant to each ship that served in Vietnamese waters.

At the end of January, I went back to the local hospital for another echocardiogram.

Present Day

These days, after having paid a visit to my local doctor I was given some good and some not so good news. The not so good was that as far as I could understand I have 2 leaking valves in my heart. The good news is that the tablets that I am taking are making a difference and the prognosis is that all is on the mend. This news has been a great lift to me, all I hope is that it keeps on mending!

Here near the end of my writings, there may be some who may well wonder why I have gone to so much trouble to put this together. As one would see there have been quite a few incidences in my life that are far from the norm and I could see that they needed recording if only for my own family to ponder on it all.

In all of my past there has always been the necessity to go forward if only at times to see what the next day will give to us all. Some of the problems were of my own making, maybe because of my own inexperience, who knows.

At the end of my time in the Navy I could show very little emotion on any subject, however it was presented to me.

Today it's almost the reverse: I show my emotions very easily, even sometimes when the sentiment has no link to me or any of my activities, it still comes out.

Several things have happened in the last couple of days that puts one's life in a different perspective. The first was when I received a letter of thanks from an unknown quarter. A pension officer of the Belmore and Oatley RSL sub branches thanked me for the contribution that my previous book had made to his client in a pension claim before a tribunal.

The other matter came out of my family history research, in regards to my forefather during his stay on Norfolk Island. I was making plans to go there myself and attempt to get some answers. Sadly, my health at that time did not allow that to happen. Although there would be very little of the Norfolk Island links that I haven't covered in my research, it would have been nice to have seen where and how they came to this part of the world.

What I must make comment on here is that I have at times been scathing of the Dept. of Veterans' Affairs. To be more correct, my criticism is directed at the legislation and the politicians that make these rules. Too often they take praise from veterans' action during service but lack the fortitude to look after that veteran when the going gets tough for that same veteran.

Let's not forget that 60,000 plus men and women served during the long Vietnam war, and it took many lives, both during that time as well as after. More often than not that war is used as a measure to the present war in Afghanistan.

Some time ago I put forward a submission with the emphasis on National Service; it was met with no response, given that I feel compelled to include it here and then it will be read by more than one person or politician. As the reader will see, I do feel strongly about this subject.

Much has been said about the role that should or would be undertaken by those whose names were drawn by the ballot system — there too was a system that had flaws. National Service is still a part of the statute books of this country, one must ask here, why? In the past, our military history tells us that our young men were called up to serve in war zones overseas, as a result of being balloted for that role and they have served in a role of another country's interest.

National Service should only be used in the defence of one's own country's borders as so defined by legislation, and yes, there should be instructions on the use of service firearms and its ancillary equipment. Here this can give rise to the teaching of many facets of what our country can do for each individual. It can offer an education system that is often out of reach of many that could fill their lives with real meaning.

Career opportunities abound out of this situation as well as a recruiting area for the permanent defence forces. Again from these sources, the investment in National Service will start to show a dividend.

As an off shoot of National Service there are several benefits, one of which is a great lead into the permanent defence forces and a way to build and sustain a well-balanced reserve force.

There is no doubt that there will be a small percentage of those unable to fit into the defence model of training, then that type of situation leads to other outlets of service during their enlistment.

Debate these days seems to be stifled by closed minds and a lack of foresight which includes a lack of thought for the younger generation and what they have to offer, these attitudes are, I'm afraid of a very selfish nature. Having served myself, one of the values that has come out of this is 'country first, self second'.

No, there was no firefight, but within the role that we undertook we sought to keep that possibility (with all its dangers) to a minimum. Those dangers will come to the fore by other researchers in due course.

There was always the question, was the other side out there watching and waiting? I would have to say "yes". Firstly, I would say I have no doubt that the Russians were there, no doubt at all.

A Russian submarine was spotted in Jervis Bay in February 1960 as well as finding another in the Tasman Sea several months earlier. The Russians had a vested interest in the Vietnam war during that time, as well as having an apparently clear understanding of Australia's defences at home and at sea.

Remember earlier we were trying to track Russian merchant ships on their way to North Vietnam. It would be a very interesting file were it to appear; the intelligence reports during those trips to Vietnam, or for that matter any intelligence file that would relate to South East Asia of that era.

As a result of my seeking input from those who served in *HMAS Melbourne* for any information that would support my proposal to the Government in Canberra, I found a man who, as a midshipman in 1962, was a part of the crew manning the emergency conning position. A part of his training as a midshipman was to keep a journal and he was required to enter in that diary events of their watch (period of duty).

From what I have gleaned so far from his documents there is a distinct pattern between 1962 and 1963. There is a lot of first-hand detail in his journal that will verify the ship's log and what is in the Report of Proceedings. There was no Sea Air Rescue ship available to facilitate the launching of fixed wing aircraft as well as no ship anti-submarine support, as I understand it had been sent to Christmas Island as a tactical move. We must remember that *HMAS Melbourne* has only 40mm antiaircraft guns, and little else in this situation and no doubt the submarine causing this situation was also aware of that as well, but I must add that were the situation to get to a point we would have launched the Sea Venoms to resolve the situation. The research so far reveals that the submarines of the Indonesian Navy were manned by Russian personnel. I am yet to be proven otherwise.

In consideration of the passive Rules Of Engagement set out for *HMAS Vendetta* in 1964, there appears to be some inconsistencies among Australian war ships operating in these areas of South East Asia, especially when you compare it with the situation there in 1963.

The late founding father of the Malay Borneo Association

of Australia told a group of us on his visit to the state branches that during his time whilst working in Darwin they had at times the experience of having Indonesian Military aircraft fly sorties as far south as Katherine. In his conversation with us he added that all these flights were of a very provocative nature. One wonders what did happen at other times during the confrontation.

On the 15th August 2009, Senator Richard Colbeck wrote a strong letter of support on my behalf, adding his emphasis as well.

On the 15th of September 2009, I wrote a letter to Dr. Kelly making him aware that his view on the matter did lack information that he failed to include for his making, in what I and many others consider as political incompetence — preach one thing and practise another.

Of course I replied to Dr. Kelly again reminding him of his reluctance to recognise the details of my submission and the reasons for that detail being documented in naval records from that particular event, with a response from his still continuing a negativity that gives the labor government a very poor record in looking after veterans.

A letter from the Vice Chief of the Defence Force, Brigadier D.A.W.Webster, Director General Nature of Service Branch had reviewed the submission and found no further evidence. What a lot of crap. I am yet to be satisfied on this matter and in due course I made a submission to the Federal Ombudsman.

In the meantime I again wrote to Brigadier Webster and

he wrote back stating the matter was closed; sounds like they may all drink from the one cup?

The response that I got from the Ombudsman gave me no joy at all; it doesn't appear that there are enough teeth in the legislation to make a just judgement. I recall that in the 1980s and onwards we had to fight very hard to get our service recorded as it should have been done.

I don't intend to give up on this one and am still planning my next move as I write this paragraph. Whilst musing over this, I re-read some of the documents that I have and found that it did happen in 1962 with *HMAS Melbourne* as well, so I have requested from the War Memorial a copy of the ship's log for that day. I wait with bated breath to see what has been written into it.

One of the most special events in my life happened on the 22nd January last, my 70th birthday. It was some 12 months in the planning by both Mary and daughter Kerrie, with granddaughter Jodi making my birthday cake; it was made to look like a golfing green with the flag of the Geelong Football Club.

Very impressive all of it, Mary had it catered for and there was more than enough to eat and drink; very special indeed.

For all the ups and downs in my life, I am still here, a little bent at times but I am still able to play 18 holes of golf and that's the part that does please me, if my golf score is anywhere near good that's an added bonus for the day.

I tend to be a bit sore next day but I'm there to see and feel those aches and pains. What is quite often said too is 'take some time' and 'smell the roses'. I do a bit of both.

Let's all hope the world is a better place for the next generation that is about to go out into the big wide world. They should also make sure that they limit the area *'where life may fall'*.

After my 70th birthday it was time to reflect on what contribution I could add to my life and to those close to me; what I have recalled is from my best memory to be factual. There would be plenty in the mix.

I have been a very true blue member of the Devonport RSL, but it saddens me that during my time as an active member of the Executive, my thoughts dwelt on the politics within, money going missing, real estate being purchased. It was sad to see this happening, but I was only one cog in the wheel, and it was hard to seek and find the guilty party. However, down the track there came stable governance which is most pleasing.

My role in the local branch of the Vietnam Veterans Association as a member took a sidestep because again there was instability within, in the main by one person who saw it as his own. This went on for several years, where in my wisdom I talked to another astute member that we needed to get back up and running and to get all our blokes back into the fold and get to work on our Vietnam Veterans' site, mindful that there is a lot to do.

That came about with a lot of persistence with the results that we were back up and running again, we had our office bearers, with myself as President and Gerald as Secretary/Treasurer. We got to work and basically set our agenda for what we could see that needed to be done. As one can imagine there would be a lot of red tape as well as ongoing negotiations ahead of us, but we stuck to it and got our membership got back up to the numbers we had previously had.

The Devonport City Council was most helpful and could see where we were coming from with foresight. We had several ideas in mind, one was a memorial wall for our veterans who have passed away since returning from their service in Vietnam. We set to work to design a wall that would meet everyone's standard with a design that set it behind our present Memorial wall and with some varied comments it was decided to keep it simple.

We then set about organising a design for the plaques which would bear each of those bloke's details which in itself would be simple, giving their name, nickname and unit that they served in. This was also extended to us who so far have survived the negatives of nature, which I made my purchase of for when I crossed the bar. Of note there are some 31 names on this wall, sadly too soon.

At a Vietnam Veterans' Memorial Service a couple of years ago mention was made to me by a state politician that the Memorial avenue would look and feel much better with a walkway through the avenue. On either side of the avenue is a plaque on a cement plinth giving brief details of the Tasmanian Vietnam Veterans who died as a result of their service while serving in Vietnam, this was erected by a Devonport Rotary group as a project. What we have been trying to do is make it a walkway of some kind through the avenue of Norfolk pines to draw visitors to that area to observe and read the plaques of each veteran.

I have researched some different means of a walkway, with the present situation still ongoing, until the Devonport City Council makes its mind up.

Early in 2006, I set about researching for details related to an incident on the 20th May 1963 with *HMAS Melbourne* making passage home from South East Asia. To get home we had to make passage through the Sunda Strait a major waterway with Indonesian territory on both sides of the strait, for this passage both *Melbourne* and *HMAS Supply* in company was a very dangerous area because Indonesia was unstable and at war within and on several of its borders.

There is much more to be said here on this issue, but I have another manuscript that provides more of my research and writings which is yet to be finished.

Just over 2 years ago I was watching the Landline program on the ABC where it showed a small town in South Australia about to close its last shop in its town, when they set to work and got murals painted on their grain silos. After some thought I put a letter in our local newspaper seeking an interest in such a project, well that has started the ball rolling with the media coming to add their bits to such a project.

I formed a committee and started to seek talks with the 2 silo owners here in Devonport; one series is for cement produced at Railton and Tas-stockfeed silos owned by a

Launceston business. I made contact with a local artist who has wide experience in this type of work. Sheffield here in Tassie is known as a mural town which has a very high visitor attendance rate.

I realise that there is a lot of planning to take place before any paint hits the surface of any silo, but first and foremost we have to get signed permission to get the ball rolling.

This has been a drawn-out affair, as our first foray got us nowhere, the grain silo were on an expansion and the cement silo people put a hold on theirs. Then along comes the COVID 19 pandemic which put everything on hold.

In mid-May I set about seeking a response from the grain silo management, but after many phone calls and emails, there was still no response whatsoever which does not go down well at all. It takes little energy to pick up the phone and ring back. We are at this time waiting with baited breath for a positive response from either.

Earlier in this memoir I talked about a very good mate, Bruce McKenzie, who sadly passed away some 5 years ago. Although he had not been well for some years he still was always a positive bloke. He was admitted to the Mersey hospital as he was not well, so his son came over from Victoria to look after him and his home. It was decided by the family to move Bruce to Victoria into a home, which happened and sadly that's where he later passed away. I still have contact with his family which is special.

In the latter part 0f 2019, Mary was not going too well. She had been going to her GP, having tests and all that goes with them. On one of her visits to the medical clinic a locum was her GP and after an ECG he read it and gave his opinion to the effect that her heart was way out of kilter and said she was very lucky as with that diagnosis she could have had a severe stroke. Since then we have had many trips to the cardiologist and to her GP with many tests and changes to her medication, with at last some improvement on the horizon.

Bad news met us this morning with our dog, Buster, not looking very well, he being 15 in dog years tells the story. He has been my right hand, very intelligent and loved kids and their attention to him, so it one of the toughest job I have had to do for a long time to take him to the vet and have him put down, as he was so much a part of our lives. He talked to us with his eyes and body gestures. My thought here is that the love and respect he gave everyone it would be so nice if the people of this world could share the same, or at least give it a try.

Ongoing from the COVID 19 virus which has restricted our movements, there has been hope that the world population may make changes to attitudes regarding race, religion and politics, but sadly that would be asking far too much. Having served in the RAN none of that was ever in our day's activities, mateship was the key and when all said and done mateship fitted in very well.

Appendix

REPORT TO FLAG OFFICER COMMANDING AUSTRALIAN FLEET by FLEET MEDICAL OFFICER.

Reference: MELBOURNE'S REPORT OF PROGRESS For APRIL, 1966, Para 31

Records of daily attendance without admission are not kept. Therefore it is not possible to make a comparison between 1965 and 1966. However I feel confident in stating that the average daily attendance has been higher in 1966 than 1965 over the comparative period of service in the strategic reserve.

2. During April the ship picked up a viral infection in Singapore which spread rapidly in the ship and affected all levels of the Ship's Company.

3. It is considered that there are 2 reasons for this:

Partial recirculation of the refrigerated air in office compartments especially on 5 deck. Upper respiratory tract infections are one of the occupational hazards of service in air-conditioned ships. This fact is supported by the experience of medical officers in such ships in HMA fleet, especially in Perth.

To check this fact I visited Surgeon Lieutenant Commander Blackstone, R. in HMS Devonshire whilst in Singapore.

He confirmed my experience and stated that at least half the Ship's Company was affected at one time or other.

This infection causes a decrease in efficiency and is more of a nuisance than a specific disease.

Recirculation through the contaminated trunking is the obvious cause rather than the air refrigeration itself. Less recirculation with more introduction of fresh air would appear to be a part solution. Alternatively, re-circulated air could be sterilised by passage over ultraviolet light tubes placed in the trunking. I consider this method of sterilisation to be given consideration.

The second cause of the spread of this infection is in the confined living space in hot, poorly ventilated mess decks. For a bacterial or viral infection to assume epidemic proportions within the community of a ship there must be sufficient susceptible individuals. Normal, healthy individuals may have their resistance to disease lowered by bad living conditions. That this is the case on Melbourne there is no doubt. In the period between Singapore and Hong Kong, many were worked in hot, humid conditions with poor facilities for adequate rest and sleep. Particularly in the case of machinery space watch-keepers who have the worst working conditions in the ship.

4. <u>HEAT EXHAUSTION</u>

Some 10 cases in all occurred over a period of about one-week. One case collapsed just after going on watch at 0800hrs, following a period on watch from 2000-2359 the previous night.

He was sufficiently dehydrated to require urgent resuscitation treatment in the sick bay. All cases were among machinery space watch-keepers. Investigation of the working conditions of machinery space watch-keepers, especially in the after machinery space disclosed an ambient air temperature of 120 Degrees F. in the control position. Keeping a 4 hour watch in this position provided the individual does not have to do heavy work is dependent on the forced draft ventilation system available at the control position.

On the night in question, the ambient temperature was 130 degrees F. and the forced draft ventilation was picking up hot air exhausted into the plenum making it impossible for watch-keepers to stand in the vicinity of the ventilation outlets upon which they are dependent for working in these conditions.

The design of the after machinery space air intake

is such that under certain conditions it is possible for exhausted hot air to be picked up from the plenum by the air intake fans.

This is what happened on the night in question above.

b. Additionally, the after machinery space air intake is on the port side just under the flight deck. Exhaust fumes from aircraft engines running over the side are picked up by these intakes. Due to the large volume of air involved this is not considered to be a health hazard. However the presence of exhaust fumes in the air in the after machinery space may account for the constant complaint of headaches by watch-keepers in this space.

5. Throughout April the daily attending list was upwards of 20. Last year it was usually below 10. These are all fresh cases and do not include patients already under treatment. The complaint of the majority of these is headache, gastric upset and diarrhoea to a lesser or greater extent.

Gastric upset induces them to stop eating adequately and a vicious cycle is formed which further lowers their vitality.

Physical examination seldom discloses any specific disability.

Treatment is difficult, as it is almost impossible to weed out the malingerers who are just fed up with the ship generally.

I have no doubt in my mind that this problem is from

bad habitability in the tropics. I consider that machinery space watch-keepers messes should be given top priority for any air conditioning program. In addition I would recommend that no individual be allowed to serve in HMAS Melbourne for a period of an absolute maximum of two years.

Finally, although the incidence of these conditions was not great among aircrew, lowered vitality could be induced by the bad living conditions in squadron cabins leading to lowered efficiency with possible increase of pilot or aircrew error of judgement. This factor may become of considerable importance when operating Trackers and Sky Hawks in the future.

Signed S. Haughton
SURGEON COMMANDER RAN
Fleet Medical Officer.

Afterword

The 24th of July is now a very significant day in my remaining life, its the day we lost my wife Mary, after some two years of ill health, early on that morning I was awoken by Mary's breathing difficulty, I rang our daughter and her husband, they came around quickly and it was then decided that we should ring for an Ambulance, within a couple of minutes three men turned up and worked on Mary with their expertise clearly showing.

It was then decided to take her to the Burnie hospital emergency section, we followed the ambulance to Burnie and I was ushered into the emergency section where I was greeted by the nurses and doctors. I have to say they were all very professional and informative in everything they did, but sadly they could not help Mary. She had been unwell for some two years and in the last 12 months she had lost a lot of weight and in the end she did not have the strength to fight anymore.

The prognosis that was finally given to me was that they had tried everything, but could not fix the problem, that being a bad heart.

They made her very comfortable, so we left and went home, coming back the next day, we were very tired, some two hours after I was home the hospital rang me to tell me Mary had passed. that news took the sap out of me.

It was then that I had to ring the family and tell them the bad news, a very tough job, totally drained, its toll on me would be that sleep would not come easy for quite a while, having looked after her for those two years made it very tough, she was my rock, one special lady.

The funeral service was so special for all the family and friends that attended.

Rest in peace sweetheart, never to be forgotten.

www.ingramcontent.com/pod-product-compliance
Lightning Source LLC
Chambersburg PA
CBHW041957080526
44588CB00021B/2767